Implementing Linkerd Service Mesh

Add Observability, Load Balancing, Micro Proxies, Traffic Split and Multi-Cluster Communication to Kubernetes

Kimiko Lee

GitforGits

ASIAN PUBLISHING HOUSE

Copyright © 2024 by GitforGits

Published by: GitforGits
Publisher: Sonal Dhandre
www.gitforgits.com
support@gitforgits.com

Printed in India

First Printing: January 2024

ISBN: 978-8119177448

Cover Design by: Kitten Publishing

For permission to use material from this book, please contact GitforGits at support@gitforgits.com.

Prologue

Cloud computing and network administration have gone a long way, and I am both excited and amazed by this fact as I sit down to write this journey. This book, my attempt to explain the world of service meshes with a deep dive into Linkerd in the possible smallest book size, is the result of countless hours spent in the trenches of network operations and a desire to demystify complex systems.

When I first learned about a service mesh, it was a revelation. The challenges of managing microservices-based architectures were growing, and the solutions were frequently as complicated as the problems. Linkerd, a service mesh, promised to not only ease these issues, but also turn them into possibilities for efficiency, security, and observability.

This book is the result of many experiences, a voyage through the complex paths of managing microservices with Linkerd. It is intended for people on the front lines of network and cloud operations - DevOps teams, networking specialists, and cloud enthusiasts - who want to use the power of service meshes. But it's more than just a technical reference. It's a transformational story about how technology can change the way we approach challenges and solve them.

Each chapter of this book peels back a layer of the service mesh ecosystem, providing useful insights and hands-on advice. This book covers everything from the principles of service meshes to the architectural subtleties of Linkerd, as well as deploying, protecting, and optimizing your network environment. The investigation into Rust programming for micro proxies is more than simply a technical deep dive; it demonstrates the changing nature of network programming.

It is my sincere wish that you will gain not only practical experience and expertise, but also a fresh outlook on the problems faced by those working in the dynamic field of cloud-native technologies as we set out on this adventure together. This book is more than simply pages of knowledge; it is a gateway to a new world of network administration possibilities, as well as a step toward mastering the art of service meshes with Linkerd.

Content

Preface

This capsule book is designed to provide DevOps teams, Networking Professionals, and Cloud Enthusiasts with the practical knowledge and skills required to set up and operate a robust service mesh with Linkerd. The book begins by demystifying the concept of service meshes, building a solid basis with an analysis of their evolution, key concepts, and the issues they face in modern cloud-native systems. It digs into Linkerd's architecture, explaining its components, features, and the seamless orchestration of microservices communication that it enables.

As readers progress through the chapters, they are taken step by step through the installation and configuration of Linkerd. The book focuses on actual implementation, guiding readers through imperative and declarative methods to ensure a complete comprehension of the setup process. The following chapters cover advanced subjects such as safeguarding interservice communications, configuring secure multi-cluster links, and implementing zero-trust authorization schemes in Kubernetes clusters. Topics includes how to organize services within Linkerd, manage error handling, retries, and timeouts, and implement effective multi-cluster communication and rollout strategies.

A key chapter is about Rust programming, emphasizing its importance in developing efficient and secure micro proxies. Readers learn how to construct, integrate, and optimize these proxies to improve their service mesh deployment.

The journey's conclusion provides readers with not only theoretical information, but also a hands-on comprehension of Linkerd. They become well-prepared to work around progressive delivery, high availability, and integration with a variety of cloud settings and tools. This book serves as a complete guide, transforming its readers into skilled architects of Linkerd-based service mesh solutions, prepared to face the dynamic challenges of modern cloud-native infrastructures.

In this book you will learn how to:

- Grasp the essentials of service mesh technology, focusing on Linkerd's transformative role in it.
- Uncover the architecture of Linkerd, understanding its components and operational dynamics.
- Master the installation and configuration of Linkerd, ensuring a seamless setup process.
- Learn to secure interservice communication, enhancing the reliability and safety of your network.
- Explore multi-cluster communication strategies, enabling robust and efficient service interactions.
- Delve into Rust programming for building high-performance, secure micro proxies in

Linkerd.

- Gain insights into advanced traffic management using Linkerd for optimal service routing.
- Navigate the intricacies of progressive delivery for deploying updates with minimal user impact.
- Discover the power of high availability in service meshes, ensuring uninterrupted service.
- Develop proficiency in integrating and optimizing linkerd2-proxy, harnessing its full potential.

GitforGits

Prerequisites

Working around Linkerd is most sought by cloud professionals, DevOps team, network professionals, platform engineers, kubernetes users and all other IT professionals working around microservices in a complex setup.

Codes Usage

Are you in need of some helpful code examples to assist you in your programming and documentation? Look no further! Our book offers a wealth of supplemental material, including code examples and exercises.

Not only is this book here to aid you in getting your job done, but you have our permission to use the example code in your programs and documentation. However, please note that if you are reproducing a significant portion of the code, we do require you to contact us for permission.

But don't worry, using several chunks of code from this book in your program or answering a question by citing our book and quoting example code does not require permission. But if you do choose to give credit, an attribution typically includes the title, author, publisher, and ISBN. For example, "Implementing Linkerd Service Mesh by Kimiko Lee".

If you are unsure whether your intended use of the code examples falls under fair use or the permissions outlined above, please do not hesitate to reach out to us at support@gitforgits.com.

We are happy to assist and clarify any concerns.

Acknowledgement

I owe a tremendous debt of gratitude to GitforGits, for their unflagging enthusiasm and wise counsel throughout the entire process of writing this book. Their knowledge and careful editing helped make sure the piece was useful for people of all reading levels and comprehension skills. In addition, I'd like to thank everyone involved in the publishing process for their efforts in making this book a reality. Their efforts, from copyediting to advertising, made the project what it is today.

Finally, I'd like to express my gratitude to everyone who has shown me unconditional love and encouragement throughout my life. Their support was crucial to the completion of this book. I appreciate your help with this endeavour and your continued interest in my career.

CHAPTER 1: INTRODUCTION TO SERVICE MESH

Evolution of Network Communication

The Monolithic Era

In the early stages of software development, applications were mostly monolithic, meaning all their components, such as the user interface, database, and server logic, were part of a single, unified codebase. This architecture meant that network communication was primarily internal, with different modules of the application interacting through method calls within the same process.

However, this approach had its challenges. As these applications grew in size and complexity, scaling them became increasingly difficult. Simple updates required redeploying the entire application, leading to longer development cycles and reduced agility. Additionally, scaling a monolithic application often meant replicating the whole application stack, even if only one component required more resources, leading to inefficient use of resources.

Birth of Microservices

The emergence of microservices marked a significant shift in application architecture. Moving away from monolithic designs, this approach involves decomposing a large application into smaller, independently deployable services. Each microservice is focused on a specific business function, enhancing flexibility and scalability. This transition altered the nature of internal method calls, transforming them into external network communications. Microservices communicate through APIs, initially using REST and later adopting gRPC for more efficient interactions. This transition enabled each service to be developed, deployed, and scaled independently, revolutionizing software development practices.

Challenges in Microservices Era

In the microservices era, the landscape of application architecture faced a paradigm shift, introducing new complexities and challenges. The pivot to a decentralized approach, where applications consist of numerous smaller, interconnected services, brought with it a rise in network traffic. This increase in traffic wasn't just in volume but also in complexity, requiring sophisticated strategies for management and monitoring.

A critical challenge in this environment was service discovery. With services constantly scaling up or down, dynamically identifying and connecting to the correct service instance became a complex task. This dynamism, while flexible, introduced a layer of complexity to maintaining consistent connectivity.

Security and compliance concerns were amplified in this new era. The dispersed nature of services, often spread across various environments, made it difficult to enforce uniform security measures. Establishing secure communication channels between these disparate services was paramount, but doing so consistently and effectively presented a significant hurdle.

Reliability and latency became focal concerns. In a landscape where a network hiccup could disrupt the intricate web of service communications, ensuring network reliability was paramount. Furthermore, the shift from internal method calls to external network calls potentially introduced higher latency. This increase in latency could adversely affect the overall performance and user experience of applications.

Role of APIs

In microservices, APIs play a crucial role in facilitating communication between services. Initially, RESTful APIs, leveraging HTTP's simplicity and ubiquity, were widely adopted in microservices architectures. However, as the need for more efficient communication increased, technologies like gRPC gained popularity. gRPC offered advantages such as reduced payload sizes and quicker serialization, addressing the growing demand for performance optimization in service-to-service interactions. This evolution of APIs reflects the ongoing quest for efficiency and efficacy in the microservices realm.

Service Mesh: A Paradigm Shift

When applied to microservices architecture, service mesh technology signifies a major change in service communication and operation. Intelligent routing, load balancing, and service discovery have always been significant issues in the wide, interconnected network of microservices. Service meshes address these issues by delivering better, more automated traffic and service management. They make it easier to discover services, which is important in dynamic contexts where services are often scaled up or down.

In terms of security and compliance, service meshes greatly improve microservices' security posture. They manage difficult activities such as encrypting service-to-service communication and administering TLS certificates, which are often done manually and intricately. Service meshes use automatic mutual TLS (mTLS) implementations to provide strong encryption, providing safe data transport. Additionally, they provide tools for enforcing consistent security standards across all microservices, which is crucial in maintaining a secure, cohesive architecture.

The capacity to see and monitor in a service mesh environment is revolutionary. Given the complexity and volume of interactions in microservices, precise insights into each service's performance and health become critical. Service meshes offer complete observability capabilities like logging, analytics, and tracing. This observability includes the ability to track individual requests as they move through the network of services, which is extremely useful for debugging and monitoring service performance.

Service meshes give equally large resilience and fault tolerance benefits. They use patterns like retries, circuit breakers, and timeouts to handle errors gracefully. These patterns contribute to the overall system's stability and uptime by ensuring that even if individual services or network components fail, the system as a whole remains robust and responsive.

The Evolution Continues

As the cloud-native landscape evolves, Kubernetes has emerged as the cornerstone for orchestrating containerized applications. This shift has necessitated the integration of service meshes with Kubernetes, streamlining network communication and aligning it with cloud-native principles. Looking ahead, we're seeing a push towards standardizing service mesh functionalities and APIs, aiming for greater interoperability and simplified management. Furthermore, the role of service meshes is expected to transcend Kubernetes-focused environments, expanding to support a broader array of deployment models and infrastructures, signaling a future of more versatile and adaptable service mesh implementations.

Genesis of Service Mesh

Developing software architecture is the first step on the path that leads to the requirement of a service mesh. Application development was traditionally done in the form of monoliths, in which all of the application's components were woven together and deployed as a single unit. Despite its apparent simplicity, this approach had a number of significant drawbacks, most notably in terms of scalability and agility. The idea of microservices gained traction as businesses tried to find architectures that were more adaptable and scalable. Microservices architecture takes applications and divides them into smaller, more manageable services that can be deployed independently. Each of these services is responsible for a particular functionality. More scalability, simpler maintenance, and quicker deployment cycles are just some of the benefits that can be gained from utilizing this approach. In spite of this, it brought about new complications, particularly in the area of communication between services being provided.

Applications that work with microservices are made up of multiple services, which are frequently deployed in different environments. The ability to communicate with one another in a dependable and secure manner is required for these services.

Following are some of the difficulties:
- Service Discovery: Locating and communicating with the right service instance.
- Load Balancing: Efficiently distributing network traffic among service instances.
- Health Checking: Ensuring services are functioning correctly and routing traffic away from unhealthy instances.
- Security: Implementing secure communication channels and managing certificates.
- Observability: Gaining insights into performance and tracing issues across distributed services.

Why Service Mesh?

The shift towards microservices has been a major trend in software development, driven by the need for more scalable, resilient, and agile applications. The need for a service mesh arises from the inherent complexities of microservices. However, this shift has introduced a range of challenges, particularly around inter-service communication and management. This is where service meshes come in, offering solutions that are critical for efficiently running microservices. Some of the factors that led to the development of service meshes include:

Dealing with Distributed Complexity

In a microservices architecture, services need to communicate over a network, which introduces complexity and potential for failure. A service mesh manages this communication, providing reliable and secure ways for services to call each other.

Consistent and Efficient Management

With potentially hundreds of services running in an environment, enforcing policies like retries, timeouts, and access control consistently is challenging. A service mesh centralizes policy definition and enforcement, ensuring consistency across all services.

Enhanced Security Posture

As microservices often run in dynamic and distributed environments, securing each service and their interactions becomes paramount. Service meshes provide key security features such as mutual TLS for encrypted communication, thus enhancing the overall security posture of the application stack.

Observability and Control

A service mesh offers deep insight into how various services are performing and interacting. This includes metrics, logs, and tracing, which are vital for diagnosing issues and understanding the behavior of complex systems.

Challenges Addressed by Service Mesh

Service meshes were designed to address the specific challenges that arose with the widespread adoption of microservices. They offer solutions to many of the pain points experienced by organizations as they scale and evolve their applications.

Network Reliability and Performance

Service meshes provide sophisticated traffic management capabilities like load balancing, circuit breaking, and intelligent routing, which are crucial for maintaining network reliability and performance.

Enhanced Security and Compliance

By handling security at the network layer, service meshes remove the burden from individual services. This includes managing secure service-to-service communication and ensuring compliance with security policies.

Operational Efficiency

Managing a microservices architecture is complex. Service meshes simplify operational tasks by providing unified tools for deploying, monitoring, and managing services at scale.

Resilience and Fault Tolerance

Service meshes introduce patterns like retries, timeouts, and circuit breakers, which are essential for building fault-tolerant systems. They help services gracefully handle failures and maintain overall system stability.

Consistency Across Services

In a distributed system, standardizing how services interact with each other is crucial. Service meshes enforce policies consistently across all services, ensuring uniformity in security, routing, and failure handling.

Simplified Debugging and Troubleshooting

With the comprehensive observability features provided by service meshes, identifying and resolving issues becomes more manageable. They offer tools for tracing requests through the network of services, helping in pinpointing the root cause of problems.

Rise of Service Mesh

With the emergence of service mesh as a solution, various tools were developed. Among them, Istio and Linkerd are prominent. These tools have significantly influenced the way service meshes are implemented in modern cloud-native environments. Understanding their features, design philosophies, and how they address specific needs in microservices architectures is essential for anyone looking to implement a service mesh.

Istio

Istio is a robust and feature-rich service mesh tool that has gained widespread adoption in the industry. It's an open-source project initially created by Google, IBM, and Lyft. Istio's architecture is composed of two main components:

1. Control Plane: The control plane is responsible for managing and configuring the proxy servers to route traffic. Key components of the control plane include:
    - Pilot: Responsible for service discovery and for configuring the Envoy proxies at runtime.

- Galley: Manages Istio's configuration and validates the configuration settings.
- Citadel: Handles security within the service mesh, including identity and credential management.

2. Data Plane: The data plane in Istio primarily consists of Envoy proxies deployed as sidecars to Kubernetes pods. Envoy proxies intercept all inbound and outbound traffic for all services in the mesh, managing and controlling this traffic based on the configurations set in the control plane.

Istio provides advanced traffic routing features, like A/B testing, canary deployments, and blue-green deployments. Istio is ideal for complex, large-scale microservice architectures where advanced traffic management and detailed observability are critical.

It offers robust security features, including mutual TLS (mTLS) for service-to-service encryption, identity and credential management, and powerful access control policies. Organizations looking to implement a zero-trust network model would find Istio's robust security features suitable for their needs. Istio shines in its observability features, offering detailed insights into service metrics, logs, and traces. This makes it easier to monitor service health, trace the flow of requests, and diagnose issues.

Linkerd

Linkerd, the first service mesh on the market, is known for its simplicity and minimalistic approach. It's part of the Cloud Native Computing Foundation (CNCF) and is a lighter alternative to Istio. Like Istio, Linkerd has a control plane and a data plane:

1. Control Plane: The control plane in Linkerd is responsible for configuration, monitoring, and management. It includes components like:
   - Destination: Responsible for service discovery.
   - Identity: Provides service-to-service authentication to ensure secure communication.
   - Proxy Injector: Automatically injects the Linkerd proxy into your service pods.

2. Data Plane: The data plane uses lightweight Rust-based proxies. These proxies are designed to be minimal and transparent, adding as little latency as possible to service calls.

Linkerd is designed to be simple to deploy and use, requiring minimal configuration. Its lightweight design ensures minimal resource consumption and performance overhead. Linkerd provides automatic mTLS, ensuring encrypted and authenticated communication between services. Linkerd is well-suited for organizations looking for an easy-to-use, lightweight service mesh solution. It's ideal for scenarios where performance and resources are critical considerations.

While both Istio and Linkerd serve similar purposes, they cater to slightly different needs and scenarios:

- Istio offers a comprehensive set of features but at the cost of increased complexity. Linkerd, on the other hand, prioritizes simplicity and ease of use.
- Linkerd's lightweight design typically offers better performance, especially in terms of resource usage and latency, compared to the more resource-intensive Istio.
- Istio provides a broader range of features, especially for traffic management and observability. Linkerd focuses on the core features necessary for a service mesh, doing so with a minimalistic approach.

The choice between Istio and Linkerd often comes down to the specific requirements of the project. For complex, large-scale environments where advanced features are a necessity, Istio is a strong contender. On the other hand, for teams looking for a straightforward, lightweight solution that is easy to manage, Linkerd is an excellent choice.

The advent of microservices brought with it a set of challenges that traditional tools were ill-equipped to handle. A service mesh represents a significant evolution in how we approach networking and service communication in distributed systems. Service mesh technologies like Istio and Linkerd emerged as solutions to these challenges, offering a way to manage complex microservices architectures efficiently. They provide critical functionalities required for modern cloud-native applications, such as reliability, security, and observability, while abstracting the complexity away from the application code itself.

Linkerd Core Components

Linkerd is structured into two main components: the control plane and the data plane. Each plays a critical role in the operation of the service mesh.

Data Plane

Overview

The data plane in Linkerd is responsible for the actual handling of the traffic between microservices. It's made up of lightweight proxies deployed alongside each service instance, often referred to as sidecars.

Key Features

- Proxy Implementation: These proxies are built using Rust, known for its performance and safety. The choice of Rust ensures the proxies are fast and memory-efficient.
- Traffic Interception: The proxies automatically intercept all inbound and outbound traffic for the services, managing it based on configurations received from the control plane.

Functioning

- Routing and Load Balancing: Once traffic is intercepted, the proxy performs load balancing, routing, and retries. It ensures that requests are evenly distributed and rerouted in case of service failure.
- Security: The proxies automatically encrypt and decrypt requests using mTLS, providing secure communication channels between services.
- Observability: They also collect metrics such as request volumes, latencies, and success rates, which are vital for monitoring and troubleshooting.

Consider a microservices-based e-commerce application. When a user places an order, the request passes through the Linkerd proxy, which may route it to the order processing service. If the primary instance is down, the proxy can reroute to a secondary instance, ensuring resilience and reliability.

Control Plane

Overview
The control plane is the management layer of Linkerd, responsible for configuring the proxies in the data plane. It doesn't handle any traffic itself but rather maintains the overall state and configuration of the mesh.

Key Components

- Destination: Responsible for service discovery, telling proxies where to send requests.
- Identity: Manages TLS certificates for mTLS, providing each proxy with its identity.
- Proxy Injector: Automatically injects Linkerd proxies into service pods as they are created.
- Public API: Provides interfaces for observing and controlling the mesh, used by the Linkerd dashboard and CLI tools.
- Service Profile Controller: Allows defining additional per-route metrics and retry policies.

Functioning

- Configuration and Management: The control plane configures the data plane proxies, determining how they route traffic, enforce policies, and report metrics.
- Service Discovery: It dynamically informs proxies about the location of services, adapting to changes in the environment, such as services scaling up or down.
- Security Certificates: The identity component issues and rotates TLS certificates for secure, authenticated communication within the mesh.

In the same e-commerce application, suppose a new payment service is deployed. The control plane recognizes this change, updates the service discovery information, and ensures that the proxies are aware of the new service. If a policy is defined for the payment service, like a retry mechanism for failed transactions, the control plane ensures this policy is implemented in the respective proxies.

When combined, Linkerd's data plane and control plane form an efficient and reliable service mesh. The control plane manages and configures the mesh to ensure it runs successfully and follows to policies, while the data plane concentrates on fast and secure traffic handling. Because of this separation of roles, Linkerd is able to be both small and powerful, meeting the complex and ever-changing needs of contemporary microservices architectures.

Service Mesh in Modern Cloud Environment

Within the context of modern cloud settings, the service mesh has evolved into an essential component, playing a significant part in ensuring the seamless operation, management, and scalability of applications. Due to the inherent intricacies of cloud-native ecosystems, the application of service mesh in these settings is diverse and solves a range of demands that occur as a result of these ecosystems.

Enhancing Cloud-Native Applications

Facilitating Microservices Architecture
Service meshes excel in environments where applications are broken down into numerous microservices. They simplify the management of these services by providing a unified layer for handling communication, security, and monitoring.

In the cloud, where services are often ephemeral and dynamic, a service mesh's ability to dynamically manage service discovery is vital. It keeps track of services as they are created, updated, or removed, ensuring seamless communication.

Simplifying Deployment and Scalability
Service meshes automatically distribute traffic among multiple instances of a service, enhancing the application's ability to handle increases in load and facilitating horizontal scaling.

They integrate deeply with container orchestration platforms like Kubernetes, automating tasks like proxy injection and managing service-to-service communication in a containerized environment.

Security in a Distributed Environment

Consistent Policy Enforcement
One of the biggest challenges in cloud environments is enforcing consistent security policies across numerous services. A service mesh centralizes this process, applying uniform security rules across all communications.

With mutual TLS, service meshes provide end-to-end encryption for all internal communications, a critical requirement in cloud environments where data breaches and leaks are a significant risk.

Identity and Access Management

In a service mesh, each service is given a unique identity, which is used in securing communication. This identity-based approach aligns well with cloud security best practices.

It allows for fine-grained access control policies, determining which services can communicate with each other, an essential aspect of maintaining security in a microservices architecture.

Operational Excellence in the Cloud

Observability and Monitoring

Service meshes provide detailed telemetry data for all service interactions. This data includes metrics on latency, request volume, error rates, and more, crucial for monitoring the health and performance of cloud applications.

They facilitate distributed tracing, a must-have in cloud environments to track the journey of requests across various services, helping in debugging and optimizing application performance.

Simplifying Complex Operations

In the cloud, networking can become complex due to the sheer number of services and their interactions. Service meshes abstract and manage this complexity, providing easy-to-use interfaces for handling networking tasks.

They incorporate resilience patterns like retries, circuit breakers, and timeouts, ensuring that cloud applications remain robust and highly available.

Multi-Cloud and Hybrid Environments

Consistent Across Environments

For organizations using multi-cloud or hybrid environments, service meshes offer a consistent layer that works uniformly across different cloud providers. This uniformity simplifies managing applications that span multiple clouds.

They enable secure and efficient communication across different cloud environments, a critical requirement for multi-cloud strategies.

Cloud Vendor Agnosticism

By providing a consistent layer across different environments, service meshes help avoid vendor lock-in, giving organizations the flexibility to choose or change their cloud providers without significant reconfiguration.

DevOps and Agile Methodologies

Enhancing Continuous Delivery

In cloud environments where continuous deployment is a common practice, service meshes support advanced deployment strategies like canary releases, blue-green deployments, and A/B testing.

They can be integrated into CI/CD pipelines, automating the deployment and management of services, which is a cornerstone of DevOps practices.

Collaboration and Efficiency

By providing common tools and interfaces for different aspects of application management, service meshes help break down silos between development and operations teams, fostering a more collaborative and efficient workflow.

Future Trends and Evolution

Service Mesh in Serverless Environments

As serverless computing continues to grow in cloud environments, service meshes are evolving to manage and secure the communication in these ephemeral and highly dynamic architectures.

AI and Machine Learning Integration

Future developments in service mesh may include more adaptive and intelligent networking and security features, potentially integrated with AI and machine learning, to further optimize and secure cloud-native applications.

The role of service mesh in contemporary cloud environments is multi-faceted, and it addresses the specific issues that are associated with these ecosystems. Service meshes have become an essential component of the cloud-native environment for a variety of reasons, including the enhancement of microservices management, the guarantee of robust security, the assistance of operational excellence, and the availability of support for multi-cloud strategies. The complex inter-service connections are not only simplified and secured by them, but they also enable enterprises to fully harness the benefits of the cloud, which in turn fosters creativity and agility in the process of developing and deploying applications.

Case Study: Realized 10x Output using Linkerd

Entain Australia, a prominent sports betting and gaming company, serves as an excellent case study for the effective utilization of Linkerd in a Kubernetes cloud-native environment. Their journey with Linkerd is a testament to the power and efficiency of this service mesh in addressing critical challenges in high-demand, data-intensive applications.

Entain Australia Overview

Entain operates globally with well-known brands like Ladbrokes and Coral. The company is listed on the FTSE 100 and employs over 24,000 people across more than 20 countries. In the fast-paced world of sports betting, latency isn't just a technical issue; it has direct financial implications. When events occur, such as a goal by Messi, the data needs to be processed and reflected in pricing systems within milliseconds, especially challenging given the geographical distance from many events.

Challenges Prior Linkerd Adoption

Entain Australia built a modern, cloud-native data feed processing platform leveraging Kubernetes, gRPC, containers, and a microservices approach. This setup, while high-performing and scalable, wasn't without its issues as below:

- The interaction between Kubernetes and gRPC caused uneven load distribution, leading to some parts of the system being overburdened ("hot") while others underutilized ("cold"). This imbalance affected the customer experience and posed a financial risk.
- The load balancing inefficiency necessitated exceptionally large servers to handle traffic volumes and limited horizontal scaling, preventing optimal use of AWS spot instances.
- The company's Kubernetes clusters span multiple AWS Availability Zones (AZs) for high availability. However, at Entain's scale, cross-AZ traffic introduced significant latency and incurred extra charges.

Implementation of Linkerd

To address these challenges, Entain Australia turned to Linkerd. They chose Linkerd for primarily these two reasons:

- Kubernetes-Native Compatibility: Linkerd seamlessly integrated with their existing Kubernetes architecture without necessitating significant changes or additional complexity.
- Ease of Installation and Low Overhead: The installation and configuration of Linkerd were straightforward, taking only a few hours for migrating 300 services to the mesh. Post-installation, Linkerd required minimal attention, aligning with the team's need for an easy-to-maintain solution.

The introduction of Linkerd brought immediate and significant benefits:

- Improved Load Balancing and Throughput: Linkerd's advanced load balancing capabilities, particularly its gRPC-awareness, immediately rectified the load balancing issues. This enhancement allowed Entain to increase their platform's request handling capacity by over tenfold.

- Optimized Horizontal Scaling and Reduced Costs: With better load balancing, Entain could leverage horizontal scaling more effectively, utilizing a broader range of smaller AWS spot instances. This shift led to substantial reductions in compute costs.
- Reduced Cross-AZ Traffic and Lower Latency: Linkerd's intelligent routing, which uses an exponentially weighted moving average (EWMA) algorithm, kept more traffic within a single AZ, thus reducing cross-AZ traffic. This change not only cut down on latency but also significantly reduced bandwidth costs.
- Overall Performance Enhancement: The deployment of Linkerd led to evenly distributed loads, faster response times, and a more stable and efficient operation across the board. The bandwidth usage and CPU load leveled out, showing a marked improvement in system performance.
- Operational Simplicity: Despite the scale of their operation (over 3,000 pods in a single Kubernetes namespace), the management of Linkerd required minimal effort, effectively like a utility service that runs in the background without needing constant attention.

Business and Operational Benefits

The most significant business benefit for Entain was the dramatic increase in platform capacity, allowing them to process a much higher volume of requests efficiently. This increase directly influenced their ability to handle betting activities, directly impacting revenue and customer experience.

From an operational standpoint, the team at Entain Australia gained peace of mind. The stability and reliability brought by Linkerd meant fewer middle-of-the-night alerts and disruptions, contributing to better work-life balance and job satisfaction.

The case study of Entain Australia shows how Linkerd may dramatically improve the performance, scalability, and operational effectiveness of a large-scale cloud-native application. Linkerd improved Entain's platform's technical capabilities while also adding significant commercial value by tackling crucial concerns such as load balancing, scalability, and cross-AZ traffic. This instance demonstrates the transformative power of implementing an appropriate service mesh in complicated and demanding cloud-native contexts.

Case Study: Scaling Cloud-Native Applications

One way to understand how service mesh technology can be applied at scale in a high-demand, cloud-native gaming environment is to look at the case study of Xbox Cloud Gaming's implementation of Linkerd. The use of Linkerd to secure and manage communications across a large network of services and pods makes this case study stand out.

Microsoft's Xbox Cloud Gaming Overview

Xbox Cloud Gaming, a part of Microsoft's gaming services, offers a catalog of hundreds of games available in 26 markets worldwide. The service has attracted over 10 million users, presenting significant infrastructure challenges due to the scale and real-time requirements of online gaming.

Infrastructure Challenges Prior Linkerd

Xbox Cloud Gaming operates an extensive infrastructure comprising 26+ Kubernetes clusters across several Azure regions, with each cluster hosting 50+ microservices and 700 to 1,000 pods. This setup totals around 22,000 pods, all of which needed to be secured and efficiently managed.

The challenges included:
- Managing thousands of pods across numerous clusters and ensuring consistent, secure, and efficient communication between these services.
- The need for a solution that could facilitate reliable, progressive deployments, such as canary releases.

Adopting Linkerd

The team at Xbox Cloud Gaming first encountered the concept of service mesh at KubeCon + CloudNativeCon NA 2018. Initially, the complexity and infancy of service mesh technology made adoption seem challenging. However, as the infrastructure continued to grow and the need for better controls and visibility became apparent, the team decided to reevaluate service mesh solutions in 2019. This revaluation was in line with their goal to improve the reliability of their infrastructure, especially for progressive deployments.

In 2020, after evaluating various service mesh solutions including Istio, Linkerd, and Consul Connect, the Xbox Cloud Gaming team chose Linkerd. Their decision was based on several criteria:
- Ensuring the solution is aligned with the Service Mesh Interface for compatibility and standardization.
- Efficient Resource Utilization as it is critical for handling the large scale of their deployment.

Implementation and Benefits

Easy mTLS Implementation

The team had previously developed an in-house mutual TLS solution for secure in-service communication. Linkerd provided a more robust, zero-config mTLS solution, saving significant engineering time and effort.

Enhanced Deployment and Monitoring

Using Linkerd, along with other CNCF projects like Flagger, Prometheus, and Grafana, the team automated canary deployments. This automation reduced the risks of downtime and allowed for faster, more confident feature rollouts.

The adoption of Linkerd reduced latency by an average of 100ms and saved thousands of dollars monthly on pods and container monitoring.

Linkerd's telemetry provided insights into request volumes, success/failure rates, and latency distributions, which were critical for monitoring and troubleshooting.

The collaboration between Linkerd and Xbox Cloud Gaming showcases the many benefits of a service mesh for enterprise-level, cloud-native applications. In addition to slashing costs and improving operating efficiencies, the team also secured communications across thousands of pods, simplified deployment, and improved monitoring. This case study highlights the importance of service meshes such as Linkerd in intricate, heavily-trafficked settings where dependability, performance, and security are of utmost importance.

Summary

This chapter has given us a thorough grasp of the service mesh ecosystem and its crucial significance in current software architectures. We began by looking into the concept of service mesh, discovering its origins in the context of the transition from monolithic to microservice architectures. While this change improved flexibility and scalability, it also created new challenges such as service discovery, load balancing, health checks, security, and observability. Service meshes arose as a response to these difficulties, serving as a specialized infrastructure layer that enables quick, dependable, and secure service-to-service communication.

We then looked at the architectures of two popular service mesh technologies, Istio and Linkerd, noting their different approaches and features. Istio's broad collection of features provides superior traffic control and detailed observability, making it ideal for complicated, large-scale systems. Linkerd, on the other hand, is praised for its simplicity, performance, and ease of use, appealing to those looking for a lightweight and uncomplicated solution. The chapter emphasized the necessity of these tools in addressing the intricacies and operational issues inherent in microservices systems.

Furthermore, extensive case studies demonstrated Linkerd's real-world uses and benefits. We looked at how Entain Australia used Linkerd to enhance platform capacity by tenfold, improve load balancing, and minimize operational expenses. Another intriguing example was Xbox Cloud Gaming, which used Linkerd to secure and manage communication across thousands of pods, streamline deployment processes, and improve monitoring capabilities in a large-scale, cloud-based gaming environment. These case studies not only demonstrated Linkerd's actual applications, but also highlighted its revolutionary impact on improving operational efficiency, scalability, and performance in complex and demanding cloud-native systems.

Overall, the first chapter provided a solid basis for understanding service meshes, with a special emphasis on Linkerd's capabilities and their use in real-world applications. This knowledge is essential for anyone wishing to set up or maintain a service mesh in modern cloud-native environments, ensuring that applications are safe, visible, and highly reliable.

CHAPTER 2: LINKERD ARCHITECTURE: UP AND RUNNING

Introduction to Linkerd Architecture

Overview

Building on the previous chapter's overview of the control and data planes, this one delves further into the inner workings of Linkerd's architecture. An elegantly built service mesh solution, Linkerd is ideal for cloud-native apps due to its lightweight, efficiency, and security. This section will explain how the system is put together and how each part works.

You can break down Linkerd's architecture into its component parts, and each one contributes something special to the service mesh. Together, they provide Linkerd's comprehensive set of features, including security, observability, and traffic management.

Components of Control Plane

Destination Service

A critical component of the control plane, the destination service plays a vital role in service discovery. It assists the data plane proxies in understanding where to route requests and the expected TLS identity of the destination. This service is also instrumental in fetching policy information, which is central to controlling the types of requests allowed, and service profile information that informs per-route metrics, retries, and timeouts.

Identity Service

Functioning as a TLS Certificate Authority, the identity service is responsible for accepting CSR (Certificate Signing Requests) from proxies and issuing signed certificates. These certificates are vital for implementing mTLS (mutual TLS) between proxies, enhancing the security of proxy-to-proxy connections.

Proxy Injector

Operating as a Kubernetes admission controller, the proxy injector is invoked every time a pod is created. It inspects resources for a Linkerd-specific annotation (linkerd.io/inject: enabled). When present, the injector modifies the pod's specification to include the proxy-init and linkerd-proxy containers, along with necessary configurations.

Components of Data Plane

Linkerd2-Proxy

The heart of the data plane, Linkerd2-proxy, is an ultralight, transparent micro-proxy written in Rust. Tailored for service mesh use, it's not a general-purpose proxy but specifically designed for the unique requirements of a service mesh. Its features include transparent proxying for HTTP, HTTP/2, TCP protocols, WebSocket proxying, automatic Prometheus metrics export, latency-aware load balancing, and automatic TLS.

Linkerd Init Container

This is a Kubernetes init container that is added to each meshed pod. It executes before any other containers start and uses iptables to redirect all TCP traffic to and from the pod through the proxy. The linkerd-init container ensures that the traffic is appropriately intercepted and managed by the proxy.

Interplay of Components

Pod Creation and Proxy Injection

When a new pod is deployed in a Kubernetes cluster with Linkerd enabled, the proxy injector component immediately comes into play. As the pod is created, the injector automatically injects the linkerd-proxy container into the pod. This is done transparently, requiring no manual intervention from the developer or administrator.

Alongside linkerd-proxy, the linkerd-init container is also injected. This init container configures iptables rules to redirect inbound and outbound traffic from the pod to go through the Linkerd proxy. This ensures that all the traffic is managed by Linkerd, providing a consistent layer for handling communication.

Service Discovery and Routing

Once the pod starts receiving traffic, the Linkerd proxy needs to determine where to send each request. This is where the destination service of the control plane plays a crucial role. It provides the proxy with the necessary information about the destination services, including their addresses and the load they're currently handling.

The destination service keeps track of the Kubernetes cluster's state, updating the proxies as services scale up or down. This dynamic response ensures that the load balancing remains efficient and effective, even as the environment changes.

Secure Communication

When a Linkerd proxy establishes a connection with another proxy, the identity service comes into play. It ensures that each proxy has a valid certificate, enabling mutual TLS (mTLS) for secure and encrypted communication between services.

The identity service automatically manages the lifecycle of the certificates, issuing, renewing, and revoking them as necessary. This automated process relieves the developers and administrators from manual certificate management.

Sample Usecase: Handling a User Request

Consider a user accessing a web service in a Kubernetes cluster managed by Linkerd. When the user sends a request:

- The request first hits the Linkerd proxy of the web service pod, redirected by iptables rules set up by the linkerd-init container.
- The proxy queries the destination service to determine the optimal service instance to handle the request.
- The proxy establishes a secure mTLS connection with the chosen service instance's proxy.
- If the request needs to be forwarded to another service, the proxy makes load-balanced routing decisions, again consulting the destination service.

Throughout this process, the proxy collects metrics on the request, which are then available for monitoring and analysis. Each component is finely tuned to perform its role within the broader context of the service mesh, ensuring that applications running within the mesh are fast, reliable, and secure. This comprehensive architecture not only addresses the inherent complexities of modern microservices-based applications but also aligns with the evolving needs of cloud-native environments.

Service Discovery in Linkerd

Essence of Service Discovery

Service discovery is a fundamental aspect of Linkerd's functionality, ensuring seamless communication within a microservices architecture. While we touched on it briefly in the context of Linkerd's architecture, a detailed exploration will provide a deeper understanding of how Linkerd handles service discovery and its significance in managing complex service interactions.

In a microservices environment, particularly in dynamic orchestration platforms like Kubernetes, services are constantly being created, moved, and terminated. This fluidity poses a challenge: how does one service know where to send a request to reach another service? This is where service discovery comes into play. It's a process that helps services dynamically discover and locate other services within the same network.

How Linkerd Manages Service Discovery?

Integration with Kubernetes

Linkerd takes advantage of the existing Kubernetes service abstraction. A Kubernetes service is a stable address for a dynamic set of pod instances providing the same function. When a service in the mesh wants to call another service, it sends the request to the stable service address.

Linkerd's control plane monitors the Kubernetes API for changes in services and pods. When a new pod is added to a service, Linkerd's control plane becomes aware of this new pod and its IP address.

The Role of the Destination Service

Dynamic Service Updates: The destination service in Linkerd's control plane plays a critical role in service discovery. It watches for changes in Kubernetes services and pods, updating the data plane proxies with the latest information about where to send requests.

Intelligent Traffic Distribution: Beyond just providing the addresses of service instances, the destination service informs proxies about the load on each instance, allowing for intelligent, latency-aware load balancing.

Service Discovery in Action

When a Linkerd-enabled pod attempts to communicate with another service, below is what happens:

DNS Resolution

The pod makes a DNS request for the service (e.g., orders.service.namespace.svc.cluster.local). Kubernetes resolves this to a stable IP, which is the virtual IP of the Kubernetes service.

Proxy Intercepts Request

The Linkerd proxy in the pod intercepts this request. Instead of sending it directly to the resolved IP, the proxy sends a request to Linkerd's destination service to get the real-time list of pod IPs that are part of the target service.

Destination Service Response

The destination service responds with a list of pod IPs, along with additional metadata like their load and health status.

Proxy Routes the Request

The Linkerd proxy then routes the request to one of these pods, taking into account the load and health information to balance the traffic effectively.

Handling Failure and Load

An essential aspect of service discovery in Linkerd is how it handles failure and load:

- Linkerd does not just perform simple round-robin load balancing. Instead, it considers the health of each service instance. If a pod is unresponsive, Linkerd will stop sending traffic to it, rerouting to healthy instances.
- Linkerd's proxies are aware of the latency to each instance. This information allows them to route requests in a way that optimizes response times, improving the overall user experience.

By abstracting the complexities of service discovery, Linkerd allows developers to focus on building their applications without worrying about the underlying network topology. Linkerd's service discovery mechanism enhances the resilience and scalability of applications. Services can scale up or down, and the mesh will automatically adjust, ensuring uninterrupted and efficient communication.

Linkerd's integration with Kubernetes makes its service discovery both effective and unobtrusive, requiring minimal configuration and intervention from the user. The intelligent routing based on load and latency ensures that applications perform optimally, balancing efficiency and resource usage.

Overall, service discovery in Linkerd is a prime example of the sophistication and efficiency that a service mesh can bring to a cloud-native environment. This functionality is crucial in today's dynamic and demanding digital landscape, where the speed and reliability of service interactions directly impact the success of cloud-native applications.

Load Balancing and Traffic Splitting

For efficient and high-availability traffic management in microservices architectures, load balancing and traffic splitting are two of Linkerd's most important features. Although these topics were briefly learned in a previous chapter, a thorough investigation will shed light on how Linkerd incorporates these features.

Load Balancing in Linkerd

Load balancing is the process of distributing network traffic across multiple servers or service instances. This is essential in a microservices environment to prevent any single instance from becoming overloaded and to ensure high availability and fault tolerance.

It is vital to know how Linkerd implements load balancing as below:

Client-Side Load Balancing
Linkerd performs client-side load balancing. When a Linkerd proxy receives a request destined for a service, it decides which service instance will handle the request. This decision is made dynamically, based on real-time data.

Service Discovery Integration
The integration with service discovery (learned previously) plays a key role. When the proxy queries the destination service for the addresses of service instances, it also receives data about their load.

Latency-Aware Balancing

Unlike traditional load balancers that might use simple round-robin or random selection, Linkerd's load balancing is latency-aware. It takes into consideration the response times of service instances, prioritizing those with lower latencies. This ensures that traffic is not just distributed evenly but also sent to the fastest-responding instances, optimizing overall performance.

Automatic Retries and Timeouts

Linkerd can also be configured to automatically retry failed requests. This, combined with load balancing, increases the resilience of the system. Linkerd's intelligent load balancing ensures that retries do not overwhelm specific service instances.

Linkerd's Traffic Splitting

Traffic splitting is another crucial feature in modern service meshes. It refers to the ability to divide traffic between different versions of a service, which is particularly useful for canary deployments, A/B testing, and blue-green deployments.

Similar to load balancing, it is of utmost importance to know the implementation of traffic splitting in linkerd as below:

Service Profiles

Linkerd uses Service Profiles to define how traffic should be split. A Service Profile is a custom Kubernetes resource that specifies configurations for a service, including routes and traffic split rules.

Splitting Traffic Between Services

The traffic split configuration allows specifying the percentage of traffic that should go to different service versions. For instance, in a canary deployment, you might start by sending 10% of traffic to the new version of a service and gradually increase it as you gain confidence in the new version.

Fine-Grained Control

Traffic splitting in Linkerd is fine-grained, meaning it can be applied not just at the service level but also at the route level within a service. This allows for more sophisticated testing and deployment strategies.

Real-Time Updates

As with load balancing, traffic splitting decisions are dynamic and can be updated in real-time without restarting pods or redeploying services. This agility is crucial for fast-paced development environments and continuous deployment practices.

Both, load balancing and traffic splitting are not just ancillary features but are core to its functionality as a service mesh. These features, powered by real-time data and seamlessly integrated with Kubernetes, offer the flexibility, dependability, and efficiency required in modern, dynamic environments. Linkerd's load balancing and traffic splitting capabilities are invaluable tools for developers and operators in cloud-native ecosystems, whether they are used to safely roll out new features with canary releases, conduct A/B tests, or simply ensure even and efficient traffic distribution.

Metrics, Logs and Dashboard

Observability in Linkerd, particularly for metrics and logs, is an important component that we have yet to investigate in depth. Linkerd's observability method is intended to provide detailed insights into the behavior of services inside a mesh while requiring minimal configuration and overhead. This capability is critical for monitoring the health and performance of apps and promptly diagnosing issues.

Metrics in Linkerd

Automatic Metrics Collection

Linkerd automatically collects a wide range of metrics for all the traffic that passes through its proxies. It integrates with Prometheus, a popular open-source monitoring solution, to store and query these metrics. This seamless integration provides real-time, detailed insights into the performance and health of applications.

The metrics collected include request volumes, success rates, request latencies, and more. These are collected on a per-service, per-route, and even per-instance basis, offering a granular view of the system.

Golden Metrics

1. Four Golden Signals: Linkerd focuses on the four golden signals of monitoring: latency, traffic, errors, and saturation. These metrics are essential for understanding the state of a system and are prominently displayed in Linkerd's dashboard.
2. Latency Metrics: These include request/response times and distributions, helping to identify performance bottlenecks.
3. Traffic Metrics: These metrics provide insights into the volume of requests handled by services.
4. Error Metrics: Tracking the rate of failed requests, these metrics are crucial for maintaining the reliability of services.
5. Saturation Metrics: These metrics give an indication of how "loaded" a service is, which can be useful for scaling decisions.

Proxy Logs

Each Linkerd proxy produces detailed logs of its operations. These logs are invaluable for troubleshooting issues like routing problems, failed requests, or unexpected behavior in the mesh.

The verbosity of proxy logs can be configured, allowing operators to balance the detail level with the volume of log data generated.

Observability Tools in Linkerd

Linkerd Dashboard

The Linkerd dashboard provides a real-time graphical view of the metrics collected by Linkerd. This includes success rates, latencies, and request volumes, all broken down by service, pod, and route. The dashboard also provides service maps, visualizing the flow of traffic between different parts of the application. This is particularly useful for understanding the dependencies and interactions between services.

Grafana Integration

Linkerd includes pre-configured Grafana dashboards for more detailed analysis. These dashboards can be customized to meet specific monitoring needs, allowing teams to focus on the metrics most relevant to their applications.

Alerting and Anomaly Detection

While Linkerd itself does not provide alerting, its integration with Prometheus enables teams to set up alerts based on the metrics Linkerd collects. This can be used for anomaly detection, notifying operators when metrics deviate from normal patterns.

The observability features in Linkerd and such level of observability is crucial in modern cloud-native environments, where understanding the behavior of distributed, dynamic systems is key to maintaining performance and reliability.

Popular Linkerd Integrations

Integrating Linkerd with existing systems enhances its capabilities and ensures a seamless and efficient operation within a broader technology ecosystem. Linkerd's design allows it to integrate with a variety of tools and platforms, enabling enhanced functionality in areas such as monitoring, security, deployment, and more. This extensive integration capability makes Linkerd a versatile and powerful tool in the cloud-native landscape.

Core Integrations

Kubernetes

Linkerd is designed to be Kubernetes-native, making it integrate seamlessly with Kubernetes clusters. It leverages Kubernetes' features like Services, Deployments, and Namespaces, aligning closely with Kubernetes' operational model.

Linkerd's integration with Kubernetes allows for automatic sidecar injection, simplifying the process of adding services to the mesh.

Prometheus and Grafana

Linkerd integrates natively with Prometheus for metrics collection. Its proxies automatically export metrics in a Prometheus-compatible format, allowing for real-time monitoring and alerting.

The integration with Grafana offers a powerful way to visualize the metrics collected by Prometheus. Linkerd even comes with pre-built Grafana dashboards for a quick and insightful view of the mesh's health and performance.

Service Mesh Interface (SMI)

Linkerd adheres to the Service Mesh Interface (SMI), a standard interface for service meshes on Kubernetes. This ensures that Linkerd can interact consistently with other tools and systems that also support SMI.

Extended Integrations

CI/CD Systems

Linkerd can integrate with various CI/CD systems like Jenkins, GitLab CI, and others. This integration can be used to automate the process of deploying and configuring Linkerd as part of the broader CI/CD pipeline.

Linkerd's traffic splitting capabilities enable it to work with CI/CD tools for canary deployments, gradually rolling out changes and assessing their impact in real-time.

GitOps Tools

Tools like Argo CD or Flux can be used in a GitOps setup to manage Linkerd configurations declaratively. This ensures that the service mesh configuration is versioned and follows the same lifecycle as the application code.

Tracing Tools

For observability, Linkerd integrates with distributed tracing systems like Jaeger and Zipkin. This integration allows for tracing requests as they move through services in the mesh, providing insights into latencies and potential bottlenecks.

Cloud Providers' Native Tools

Linkerd can integrate with cloud providers' native tools and services, such as AWS CloudWatch, Azure Monitor, and Google Cloud's operations suite, for enhanced monitoring and observability.

Network Policies and Security Tools

Integration with Kubernetes network policies and other security tools enhances the security aspect of the service mesh. This allows for defining granular access controls and security policies.

Service Discovery Tools

While Linkerd natively supports Kubernetes service discovery, it can also integrate with external service discovery tools for environments where services span multiple platforms or clouds.

API Gateways and Ingress Controllers

Linkerd can be used in conjunction with API gateways and ingress controllers like NGINX, Traefik, or Kong. This allows for managing ingress traffic effectively, applying Linkerd's features like mTLS and load balancing to incoming traffic.

Logging and Analysis Tools

Integration with log aggregation and analysis tools like ELK Stack (Elasticsearch, Logstash, Kibana) or Splunk helps in centralizing and analyzing logs generated by Linkerd proxies and applications in the mesh.

Serverless Frameworks

In serverless environments like AWS Lambda or Azure Functions, Linkerd can integrate to provide observability and routing capabilities, though this might require specific configurations due to the ephemeral nature of serverless functions.

Custom Tooling via Linkerd's API

Linkerd's API can be used to build custom integrations and tooling. This is particularly useful for organizations with specific operational requirements or those looking to integrate Linkerd into a bespoke toolchain.

Overall, the above-mentioned Linkerd integrations with existing systems and other technology stacks demonstrate its versatility and adaptability in the cloud-native ecosystem. These integrations not only broaden Linkerd's fundamental capabilities, but also ensure that it can work seamlessly in a complex, multi-tool environment, providing greater value to its customers. Linkerd's extensibility and adaptability make it an excellent solution for enterprises wishing to leverage a service mesh that integrates seamlessly with their current infrastructure and tools ecosystem.

Summary

This chapter provides a thorough overview of Linkerd's architecture, concentrating on its sophisticated yet user-friendly design. We looked at the intricate workings of Linkerd's control and data planes, which are critical to its functionality. The control plane, which includes components such as the Destination and Identity services, oversees the mesh's setup and security. The data plane, driven by the lightweight Linkerd2-proxy, handles the real traffic, ensuring efficient and secure communication among services. This division of duties enables Linkerd to provide a seamless service mesh experience, managing traffic, security, and observability with minimum overhead.

We investigated the operational dynamics of these components, demonstrating how they combine to provide a strong service mesh solution. The proxy injector component enables the automatic injection of Linkerd proxies into Kubernetes pods. The proxies then use the Destination service to perform dynamic service discovery, resulting in intelligent load balancing and efficient traffic routing. The Identity service addresses security by managing TLS certificates and enables mutual TLS (mTLS) for safe communication between services. Additionally, the Linkerd init container configures iptables rules to redirect traffic through the proxy, ensuring complete traffic control.

Furthermore, we investigated Linkerd's comprehensive integration capabilities with existing systems and technology stacks. Its operational environment is built around its native integration with Kubernetes and Prometheus, which allows for smooth service management and thorough monitoring. Linkerd also works with many CI/CD systems, tracing tools like Jaeger and Zipkin, and cloud providers' native tools to improve functionality. These connectors expand Linkerd's capabilities by enabling automated deployments, additional security measures, and extensive observability. They highlight Linkerd's adaptability and ability to integrate into various and complicated technology ecosystems, making it an indispensable tool in the cloud-native landscape.

Overall, this chapter has focused on Linkerd's architectural elegance and operational efficiency. Its architecture not only solves the inherent difficulties of current microservices-based systems, but also aligns with the changing requirements of cloud-native settings, guaranteeing that applications are fast, dependable, and secure.

CHAPTER 3: INSTALLING AND CONFIGURING LINKERD

Pre-installation and Setup Requirements

The practical aspects of setting up Linkerd in a variety of situations are the primary focus of this chapter. Before beginning the installation process, it is critical to understand the pre-installation prerequisites, which ensure that the environment is prepared for a successful Linkerd deployment. These prerequisites differ slightly depending on whether you're installing Linkerd on a Linux server, in a cloud environment, or in a hybrid.

Pre-installation Requirements

For All Environments
- Kubernetes Cluster: Linkerd requires a Kubernetes cluster to run. The cluster version should be compatible with the version of Linkerd you plan to install.
- kubectl: The Kubernetes command-line tool, kubectl, must be installed and configured to communicate with your Kubernetes cluster.
- Resource Requirements: Ensure your Kubernetes cluster has sufficient resources (CPU and memory) to host Linkerd's control plane and sidecar proxies.
- Network Connectivity: The Kubernetes cluster should have proper network connectivity. This includes outbound internet access if you're pulling Linkerd images from the web.

Additional for Linux
- Docker: If you're running Kubernetes locally on Linux (e.g., Minikube, kind), Docker needs to be installed as it's used for running containers.
- User Permissions: Ensure you have the necessary permissions to deploy applications to your Kubernetes cluster.

Additional for Cloud Environments
- Cloud Provider CLI Tools: Install and configure CLI tools for your cloud provider (e.g., AWS CLI, Azure CLI, Google Cloud SDK) for managing resources in the cloud.
- Cloud-Specific Kubernetes Setup: Some cloud providers offer managed Kubernetes services (like EKS, AKS, GKE). Ensure you're familiar with the specifics of deploying applications on these platforms.
- IAM Roles and Permissions: Configure the necessary IAM roles and permissions for deploying and managing Kubernetes resources.

Additional for Hybrid Environments
- Network Configuration: Ensure proper network connectivity and configurations between your on-premises and cloud environments.
- Consistent Kubernetes Versions: If you're running Kubernetes in both environments, ensure that the versions are compatible.

Step-by-Step Installation of Linkerd

Install the Linkerd CLI

The first step is to install the Linkerd CLI on your local machine. This CLI is used to interact with Linkerd.

```
curl -sL https://run.linkerd.io/install | sh
```

For Windows, download the executable from the Linkerd releases page.

Add the Linkerd CLI to your path:

```
export PATH=$PATH:$HOME/.linkerd2/bin
```

Validate Your Kubernetes Cluster

Before installing Linkerd, it's a good idea to ensure your Kubernetes cluster is configured correctly.

```
linkerd check --pre
```

This command checks that your cluster is compatible with Linkerd.

Install Linkerd onto the Cluster

Now, deploy Linkerd's control plane onto your Kubernetes cluster:

```
linkerd install | kubectl apply -f -
```

Verify the Installation

After installation, run the following command to ensure everything is set up correctly:

```
linkerd check
```

Install the Linkerd Dashboard

For a visual representation of Linkerd's performance, you can install the dashboard:

```
linkerd dashboard
```

This command launches a web browser interface showing various metrics and details about your services.

With these steps, Linkerd should be up and running in your Kubernetes cluster, whether it's on Linux, in the cloud, or a hybrid environment. Remember, the specifics might vary slightly based on your particular setup, but the overall process remains largely the same. The next steps involve configuring Linkerd to mesh your services, which we will cover in the upcoming sections of this chapter.

Linkerd Configuration

After you have installed Linkerd on your Linux-based Kubernetes cluster, the next step is to configure it so it can be used effectively. We shall start with a simple but vital task: injecting the Linkerd proxy into your Kubernetes services. This method adds your services to the Linkerd service mesh, allowing them to benefit from features like encrypted communication, observability, and reliability advantages.

Injecting Proxies into Kubernetes

Identify the Kubernetes Namespace

Choose the Kubernetes namespace where your services are running. If you don't have a specific namespace, you can use the default one. Do verify that the namespace is not part of the Linkerd control plane.

If you want all future deployments in a particular namespace to be automatically added to the mesh, you can annotate the namespace:

```
kubectl annotate namespace <your-namespace> linkerd.io/inject=enabled
```

Replace <your-namespace> with the name of your namespace.

Manually Injecting the Proxy for a Deployment

If you prefer to inject the proxy into specific deployments rather than at the namespace level, use the following commands. First, retrieve the YAML for your deployment:

```
kubectl get deploy <your-deployment> -o yaml > <your-deployment>.yaml
```

Use the Linkerd CLI to modify the deployment YAML:

```
linkerd inject <your-deployment>.yaml | kubectl apply -f -
```

This command adds the Linkerd proxy as a sidecar container to your deployment.

Verifying the Injection
Verify that the proxy has been added by describing the pods in your deployment:

```
kubectl describe pod -l app=<your-app>
```

You should see the linkerd-proxy container listed in the pod description.

Observing Service
If you installed the Linkerd dashboard, you can now see your service in the dashboard:

```
linkerd dashboard
```

Within the dashboard, navigate to the namespace and observe the metrics for your service. You should see data on request volume, success rates, and latencies.

Test Service Communication
Test the communication between your services to ensure they are properly interacting over the mesh. You can do this by sending requests to your services and observing the traffic in the dashboard.

Additional Configuration Options

By default, Linkerd automatically configures mTLS for all meshed services. You can observe mTLS metrics in the dashboard to ensure secure communication.

For advanced routing and observability, consider setting up service profiles, which allow you to define fine-grained routing rules and collect additional metrics.

Depending on your service's resource requirements, you may want to configure the CPU and memory resources allocated to the Linkerd proxy.

Upgrade Linkerd Version

The upgrade process in Linkerd is designed to be as smooth and disruption-free as possible. We shall walk through the steps to upgrade Linkerd on a Linux-based Kubernetes environment and how to ensure that your existing operations seamlessly transition to the new version.

Check Current Version

Before upgrading, it's good to know your current version of Linkerd. Use the Linkerd CLI to check this:

```
linkerd version
```

Update the Linkerd CLI

Ensure that your Linkerd CLI tool is updated to the latest version, as it needs to match the version of the Linkerd control plane that you plan to install.

Download and install the latest version of the Linkerd CLI from the official website or use the command line:

```
curl -sL https://run.linkerd.io/install | sh
```

Update your path (if you haven't permanently added it):

```
export PATH=$PATH:$HOME/.linkerd2/bin
```

Verify the CLI version:

```
linkerd version
```

Backup Configuration (Recommended)

It's a best practice to backup your Linkerd configuration before proceeding with the upgrade. This can be done by exporting the current configuration to a file:

```
kubectl -n linkerd get configmap linkerd-config -o yaml > linkerd-config-backup.yaml
```

Perform the Upgrade

Use the Linkerd CLI to upgrade the control plane:

```
linkerd upgrade | kubectl apply -f -
```

This command generates the Kubernetes configs necessary to upgrade Linkerd and applies them to your cluster.

Verify the Upgrade

After applying the upgrade, ensure that all components are up and running:

```
linkerd check
```

Update Data Plane Proxies

After upgrading the control plane, you'll need to update the data plane proxies (i.e., the Linkerd sidecar containers in your service pods).

You can do this by using the linkerd upgrade command:

```
kubectl get -n <namespace> deploy -o yaml | linkerd inject - | kubectl apply -f -
```

Replace <namespace> with the namespace of your services.

This command retrieves your deployments, injects the updated proxy, and re-applies the configurations.

Confirm Data Plane is Up-to-Date

Confirm that all your data plane proxies are running the updated version:

```
linkerd check --proxy
```

Once the upgrade is complete, monitor your services closely for any anomalies. Use the Linkerd dashboard to check service metrics and logs. Perform thorough testing of your application to ensure all services are functioning correctly with the upgraded Linkerd version.

By doing these steps, you may keep your Linkerd instance up to date with the most recent upgrades and security fixes. For specific information on each release, consult the official Linkerd documentation and release notes.

Troubleshooting Installation and Configuration

When installing and configuring Linkerd in a Linux-based Kubernetes environment, you may encounter various issues or errors. Understanding these common problems and knowing how to troubleshoot them is crucial for a smooth operation. Following are some typical issues, their causes, and practical solutions.

Failed to Install Linkerd Control Plane

This issue often arises due to insufficient permissions, connectivity issues, or incompatible Kubernetes cluster configurations.

Troubleshooting and Resolution
- Ensure your Kubernetes cluster is compatible with the version of Linkerd you're trying to install.
- Verify that your cluster has enough resources (CPU, memory) to host the Linkerd control plane.
- The error messages from the linkerd install command can provide clues. Look for any permission-related errors or connectivity issues.
- Ensure you have the necessary cluster roles and permissions to deploy applications.

Data Plane Proxies Not Starting

This can occur if the automatic sidecar injection fails, or if there are issues with the proxy configuration or resource limits.

Troubleshooting and Resolution
- Review the logs of the Linkerd proxy injector for errors as below:

```
kubectl -n linkerd logs deployment/linkerd-proxy-injector
```

- Ensure your namespaces or pods are correctly annotated with linkerd.io/inject: enabled.
- Check if the resource limits set for the proxies are too low, preventing them from starting.

mTLS Not Working

Issues with mTLS often stem from incorrect certificate setup or misconfiguration of the Identity service.

Troubleshooting and Resolution
- Verify the Linkerd Identity service is functioning properly.
- kubectl -n linkerd logs deployment/linkerd-identity
- Ensure that the TLS certificates are correctly issued and valid.
- The proxy logs can provide details on any mTLS-related errors.

Services Not Discovering Each Other

This issue usually arises due to misconfigurations in service discovery or DNS resolution problems.

Troubleshooting and Resolution
- Confirm that your Kubernetes DNS is configured correctly and functioning.
- Check the logs of the Linkerd Destination service for any errors.

```
kubectl -n linkerd logs deployment/linkerd-destination
```

- Ensure that the services have active endpoints and are reachable from within the cluster.

Performance Degradation After Meshing Services

Performance issues might be due to resource contention, improper load balancing, or network configuration issues.

Troubleshooting and Resolution
- Check if the nodes have sufficient resources to handle the additional load of Linkerd proxies.
- Use Linkerd's dashboard to analyze the performance metrics of your services. Look for high latencies or error rates.
- Review your network configuration for any bottlenecks or misconfigurations.

Linkerd Dashboard Not Accessible

This can occur if the Linkerd dashboard service is not properly deployed or if there are networking issues.

Troubleshooting and Resolution
- Dashboard Service State: Check the state of the dashboard service.

```
kubectl -n linkerd get svc web
```

- If using port-forwarding to access the dashboard, ensure it is set up correctly.
- Verify that no firewall or network policy is blocking access to the dashboard.

Ingress Traffic Not Being Meshed

This happens when the ingress controller or ingress resources are not properly configured to work with Linkerd.

Troubleshooting and Resolution
- Ensure that your ingress controller and resources are correctly configured to route traffic

through Linkerd proxies.
- Verify that the Linkerd proxy is injected into your ingress controller's pods if necessary.
- Review the logs of the ingress controller for any errors related to Linkerd.

Many of these difficulties may be avoided by regularly monitoring, allocating resources properly, and adhering to best practices in Kubernetes and Linkerd setups. Additionally, keeping up with Linkerd's documentation and community assistance can provide helpful insights for dealing with difficult issues.

Best Practices - Installation, Updates and Configuration

The service mesh's performance and stability can be optimized and problems can be minimized by following best practices when utilizing Linkerd in a Linux-based Kubernetes system. We shall take a look at these recommended methods and see how we can put them into action.

#1 - Gradual Rollout of Linkerd

Begin by deploying Linkerd in a non-production environment or a small section of your production environment. This approach allows you to understand how Linkerd affects your applications and infrastructure.

After installation, closely monitor the performance and behavior of your services using the Linkerd dashboard and other monitoring tools.

Once you're confident with the setup, gradually roll out Linkerd across more services and environments.

#2 - Keeping Linkerd Up-to-Date

Regularly check for new releases of Linkerd. Up-to-date versions include performance improvements, bug fixes, and security patches.

Use the Linkerd CLI to update your Linkerd installation, as it ensures compatibility between the CLI and the control/data planes.

```
linkerd upgrade | kubectl apply -f -
```

#3 - Monitoring and Alerting

Utilize the built-in Prometheus instance and Grafana dashboards provided by Linkerd for real-time monitoring.

Configure alerts in Prometheus for key metrics like high latency, error rates, or pod failures.

Frequently review the Linkerd dashboard for any anomalies or issues.

#4 - Optimal Resource Allocation

Ensure that your Kubernetes nodes have enough resources (CPU, memory) to handle the Linkerd control plane and proxies.

Set appropriate resource limits and requests for the Linkerd proxies to prevent resource contention.

```
config.linkerd.io/proxy-cpu-limit: "1"
config.linkerd.io/proxy-memory-limit: "1Gi"
```

#5 - Secure Your Service Mesh

Linkerd provides automatic mutual TLS (mTLS) for secure communication. Ensure that it's enabled and functioning correctly.

Implement Kubernetes network policies to control the traffic flow between pods for additional security.

#6 - Proper Namespace Configuration

Annotate namespaces or deployments selectively for Linkerd injection. This helps you control which parts of your application use Linkerd.

```
kubectl annotate namespace <namespace> linkerd.io/inject=enabled
```

Implementing these best practices will not only enhance the performance and reliability of your Linkerd service mesh but also ensure a secure, maintainable, and scalable infrastructure.

Summary

This chapter offered a detailed approach to configuring and managing Linkerd in a Linux-based Kubernetes infrastructure. We began with the prerequisites for installation, highlighting the need of a Kubernetes cluster that is compatible, as well as the necessary resources and network configuration. The installation method was learned step by step, with a focus on using the Linkerd CLI to install the control plane, confirm the configuration, and inject proxies into Kubernetes services. We also learned how to upgrade Linkerd, ensuring that users can effortlessly transition to newer versions while retaining the stability and performance of their service mesh.

Following installation, we learned common issues that may develop and how to resolve them. This section was critical for assessing the potential issues and educating users for successful problem-solving. We learned about a variety of concerns, including failed installations, proxy injection problems, mTLS issues, service discovery difficulty, performance degradation, dashboard accessibility, and ingress traffic issues. Each problem was followed by its causes and a set of practical techniques for diagnosing and resolving it, with a focus on log analysis, system resource checks, and configuration verification.

Finally, the chapter taught critical recommended practices for using Linkerd efficiently. These included a gradual rollout, regular updates, vigilant monitoring and alerting, optimal resource allocation, securing the service mesh with automatic mTLS and network policies, careful namespace configuration, implementing retry and timeout policies, using traffic splits for controlled rollouts, and incorporating logging and tracing tools. The value of connecting with the Linkerd community for support and ongoing learning was emphasized. This set of best practices serves as a critical checklist for creating a strong, secure, and high-performing service mesh environment, allowing users to fully utilize Linkerd's capabilities in their Kubernetes deployments.

CHAPTER 4: SECURING COMMUNICATION WITH LINKERD

Concept of Interservice Security

Overview

One of the most important parts of contemporary microservices architectures is interservice security, which is the subject of this chapter. When it comes to distributed systems, interservice security is all about the safeguards put in place to make sure that services can talk to each other safely. Separating applications into smaller, more manageable services that can be deployed independently and communicate with each other over a network is known as microservices. Interservice security is of utmost importance due to the distinct security challenges that are brought about by this distributed nature.

Interservice security encompasses various aspects, including authentication, authorization, encryption, and data integrity. It ensures that only authorized services can communicate with each other, that data transferred between services is confidential and not tampered with, and that the integrity of the communication is maintained.

Authentication

- Service Identity: In microservices, each service should have a distinct identity. Authentication involves verifying the identity of a service to ensure that communications are with the intended and trusted entity.
- Mutual TLS (mTLS): One common method to achieve service-to-service authentication is through mutual TLS, where both client and server authenticate each other using TLS certificates.

Authorization

- Access Controls: Once a service's identity is verified, authorization determines what that service is allowed to do. This involves defining and enforcing policies that control which services can communicate with each other.
- Role-Based Access Control (RBAC): This is a common approach where access rights are assigned based on the role of a service within the system.

Encryption

- Data Confidentiality: Encryption ensures that data transmitted between services is unreadable to unauthorized parties. This is crucial for protecting sensitive information from being intercepted during transmission.
- End-to-End Encryption: Ideally, encryption should be end-to-end, meaning data is encrypted when it leaves one service and remains encrypted until it reaches the destination service.

Interservice Security Challenges

Implementing interservice security in large, dynamic environments presents several challenges. The complexity arises from managing security across numerous service interactions. Additionally, implementing security mechanisms often leads to performance overhead, particularly due to the latency introduced by encryption and decryption processes. Another significant challenge is managing and rotating TLS certificates in systems using mutual TLS (mTLS), which becomes increasingly difficult with the number of services involved. Furthermore, cloud-native environments, characterized by frequent scaling of services, add complexity to maintaining consistent security across all instances.

Service meshes like Linkerd effectively address these issues by delegating interservice security to a dedicated infrastructure layer. They automate TLS certificate issuance, rotation, and revocation, removing the need for manual intervention. Service meshes ensure that security policies are applied uniformly across all services, regardless of scale. They also provide transparent traffic encryption and decryption, ensuring end-to-end security without the need for service code changes. Furthermore, service meshes incorporate advanced identity and access management features, which simplify the authentication and authorization processes for service communications.

mTLS Deep Dive

mTLS in Linkerd

One of the most important security features in Linkerd is called automatic mutual TLS (mTLS), and it helps to make communications in microservices architectures more secure. In addition to providing a double-layered identity assurance, mTLS is an advanced form of TLS that guarantees mutual authentication between parties that are communicating with one another. In the context of Linkerd's service mesh, this functionality ensures that all service interactions are authenticated and encrypted at the same time. This robust security measure provides an effective defense against attacks that involve impersonation and eavesdropping, and it plays an essential part in preserving the integrity and confidentiality of interservice communications within the mesh.

How Linkerd Implements mTLS?

mTLS is implemented by Linkerd through a process that is both seamless and automated. For all of the services that are contained within the mesh, it automatically manages TLS certificates, which is a task that is typically difficult to accomplish but is made transparent and user-friendly in Linkerd. Within Linkerd, the Identity service performs the function of a Certificate Authority, which is responsible for issuing TLS certificates to each proxy. These proxies, which serve as sidecars for each service, are responsible for handling the necessary encryption and decryption of traffic transactions. The use of mTLS, which ensures the safety of data while it is being transferred across the service mesh, takes place during this proxy-based communication setting.

Working of Automatic mTLS

Secure communications within the service mesh rely on Linkerd's complex automatic mTLS process. When a new pod becomes available, the embedded Linkerd proxy requests a TLS certificate from the Identity service. This certificate is unique to the proxy and represents the service it is associated with. After verifying the proxy's credentials, the Identity service issues the TLS certificate. Linkerd rotates these certificates on a regular basis, enhancing security due to their short lifespan and reducing the risks associated with potential compromises.

During communication, any outbound traffic from a proxy is automatically upgraded to TLS using the certificate provided by the Identity service. In contrast, for inbound traffic, the proxy validates the incoming connection's certificate to ensure it comes from a trusted service within the mesh. This entire process is executed transparently, eliminating the need for any changes to the application code and ensuring a seamless and secure communication channel within the service mesh environment.

Benefits of Automatic mTLS in Linkerd

The automatic mTLS feature in Linkerd significantly improves security within the service mesh. By requiring mutual authentication, it ensures that only verified services within the mesh communicate, thereby increasing security. This mutual authentication, combined with traffic encryption, protects sensitive information from unauthorized access. Linkerd streamlines security operations by automating certificate management, reducing manual tasks and errors. The certificate's short lifespan and automatic rotation enhance security. Furthermore, mTLS helps to comply with data security regulations and creates a trust framework within the mesh. Importantly, Linkerd maintains efficient performance despite the additional security layers, reducing latency via optimized proxies and cryptographic processes.

Challenges and Considerations

Although it improves security, implementing mTLS in Linkerd makes debugging and visibility more difficult. Normal plaintext inspection tools are rendered useless due to the encryption of traffic. The extensive metrics and logging capabilities of Linkerd, however, make this less of an issue and allow for more effective monitoring and troubleshooting.

Strategic planning is required to ensure that external services that are not part of the Linkerd mesh trust certificates issued by Linkerd's Identity service. To achieve this goal, certificate federation between meshed and non-meshed services may be necessary.

To make sure the security protocols work smoothly with Linkerd's mTLS traffic, organizations should also adjust their firewall rules to accommodate it.

Multi-Cluster Links and Its Security

Multi-Cluster Links in Linkerd

For organizations with applications spread across multiple Kubernetes clusters, perhaps across different regions or cloud providers, secure multi-cluster communication is essential. It's vital for maintaining data privacy and complying with regulatory standards. Linkerd addresses this need by facilitating secure and reliable inter-cluster service communication. It establishes encrypted and authenticated tunnels between clusters, ensuring data security in transit. Linkerd's approach to multi-cluster communication is geared towards simplicity and ease of management, allowing for straightforward cluster connections without the need for complex network setups or VPNs.

Sample Program: Establishing Multi-Cluster Links

Assume that Cluster-Alpha hosts the frontend services, while Cluster-Beta manages backend services like databases and analytics. To facilitate secure communication between these clusters, FusionCorp needs to establish a multi-cluster link using Linkerd.

To begin with, first ensure that Linkerd is installed on both Cluster-Alpha and Cluster-Beta. You can follow the installation steps covered in Chapter 3.

You also need kubectl access to both clusters and the contexts should be correctly set up in your kubeconfig file.

Setup Linkerd Multicluster Components

First, install the multi-cluster components on Cluster-Alpha (the source cluster):

```
linkerd --context=cluster-alpha multicluster install | kubectl --context=cluster-alpha apply -f -
```

Repeat the same process on Cluster-Beta (the target cluster):

```
linkerd --context=cluster-beta multicluster install | kubectl --context=cluster-beta apply -f -
```

Establish the Link Between the Clusters

Generate a manifest to link Cluster-Beta to Cluster-Alpha:

```
linkerd --context=cluster-beta multicluster link --cluster-name beta-cluster |
kubectl --context=cluster-alpha apply -f -
```

This command creates the necessary resources in Cluster-Alpha to communicate with Cluster-Beta securely.

Export Services from Cluster-Beta

In Cluster-Beta, annotate the services that you want to be accessible from Cluster-Alpha. For example, if you have a service named backend-service:

```
kubectl --context=cluster-beta annotate svc backend-service
mirror.linkerd.io/exported=true
```

This annotation makes backend-service available for mirroring from Cluster-Alpha.

Access the Service from Cluster-Alpha

In Cluster-Alpha, you can now access backend-service from Cluster-Beta as if it were a local service. Linkerd takes care of routing the requests securely to Cluster-Beta.

Security Considerations

1. mTLS Encryption: Linkerd automatically encrypts the traffic between clusters using mTLS, ensuring that the communication is secure.
2. Identity Verification: The proxies in both clusters verify each other's identities before establishing communication, preventing any unauthorized access.
3. Access Control: Regular Kubernetes RBAC and network policies can be used in conjunction with Linkerd's multi-cluster setup to control access and ensure that only authorized services can communicate across clusters.
4. Monitoring and Observability
5. Linkerd Dashboard: The Linkerd dashboard can be used to monitor the traffic between clusters. You can observe metrics such as latency, request volume, and success rates for cross-cluster requests.
6. Logs and Alerts: Regular monitoring practices, like collecting logs and setting up alerts, should be extended to include the multi-cluster setup. This helps in quickly identifying and resolving any issues that may arise.

By encrypting traffic using mTLS, this entire setup guarantees that services in different Kubernetes clusters can communicate reliably and securely. Connecting FusionCorp's Cluster-Alpha and Cluster-Beta was a breeze with Linkerd's multi-cluster communication, which allowed for secure and observable interservice communication.

Zero Trust Security

Zero trust is a security concept centered on the belief that organizations should not automatically trust anything inside or outside their perimeters. Instead, they must verify anything and everything trying to connect to its systems before granting access. This approach marks a significant shift from traditional security models which operated on the assumption that everything inside an organization's network should be trusted.

Key Principles of Zero Trust

- Never Trust, Always Verify: Zero trust requires continuous verification of the security and integrity of all interactions, regardless of their location within or outside the network.
- Least Privilege Access: Users, applications, and systems are granted only the minimum level of access necessary to perform their functions. This limits the potential damage from breaches or insider threats.
- Microsegmentation: Networks are segmented into small zones to maintain separate access for separate parts of the network. If one segment is breached, others remain secure.
- Layered Defense: Multiple layers of security controls are employed to protect data, including encryption, multi-factor authentication, and endpoint security.
- Real-time Monitoring and Response: Continuous monitoring of network and system activities to detect and respond to threats in real-time.

Zero Trust in Kubernetes Cluster

Implementing a zero-trust model in Kubernetes using Linkerd involves several key steps. These steps are designed to ensure that no traffic is trusted by default and that all communication is authenticated and encrypted, aligning with the zero-trust principles. We will continue using the example of FusionCorp, which has two Kubernetes clusters, Cluster-Alpha and Cluster-Beta, where Linkerd is already installed and configured.

Enforce Mutual TLS (mTLS) for All Services

With Linkerd, mTLS is automatically enabled and configured for all meshed services. This ensures that all communication between services is both encrypted and authenticated.

Ensure that mTLS is active for all services in both clusters. You can check the mTLS status using the Linkerd dashboard or CLI. In the Linkerd dashboard, under the "Namespaces" section, you can see if mTLS is enabled for each service.

Establishing Identity and Certificates

Linkerd's Identity service automatically issues and manages TLS certificates for all proxies, ensuring each service has a unique identity.

Do verify the Linkerd Identity service is operating correctly in both clusters. You can verify the Identity service logs for any unusual activities or errors.

Implement Strict Access Controls

Using Kubernetes' Role-Based Access Control (RBAC), enforce strict access policies for both users and services.

Create specific roles in Kubernetes that define what each service can and cannot do. Use RoleBindings to apply these roles to the specific services.

Network Policies

Implement Kubernetes network policies to control the flow of traffic between pods, ensuring that services can only communicate as per the defined policies.

Define network policies that restrict communication between services based on their requirements. Apply these policies across both clusters to ensure traffic is strictly regulated according to the zero-trust model.

Continuous Monitoring and Logging

Set up continuous monitoring and logging to detect and respond to any anomalies or security threats.

Use Linkerd's integration with Prometheus and Grafana for real-time monitoring. Set up alerts for any suspicious activities that might indicate a breach or an attempt to access services without proper authorization.

Ensure that logs from Linkerd proxies and Kubernetes are collected and monitored. Use log analysis tools to detect any potential security issues.

Regularly Update and Patch

Keep Linkerd and Kubernetes regularly updated to ensure you have the latest security fixes and improvements.

Set a regular schedule for updating Linkerd and Kubernetes. Monitor Linkerd's releases for any security patches or updates.

Audit and Compliance Checks

Regularly perform audits to ensure that the zero-trust policies are effectively enforced and comply with any regulatory standards.

Regularly review the access controls, network policies, and mTLS configurations. Ensure that they align with the organization's security policies and standards.

Implementing zero trust in Kubernetes requires the enforcement of mTLS for secure communication, strict access controls, network policies for regulated traffic flow, continuous monitoring for anomalies, regular updates, and compliance checks. Following the above said steps, you or the FusionCorp can ensure that its Cluster-Alpha and Cluster-Beta operate under a robust zero-trust model, significantly enhancing the security and integrity of their microservices architecture.

Certificates and Identity Management

Brief Overview

In Linkerd, the Identity component is responsible for managing the lifecycle of TLS certificates used for mutual TLS (mTLS) communication between services. Linkerd's Identity service automatically issues, rotates, and revokes TLS certificates for each proxy in the mesh. These certificates are used to securely identify and authenticate services to each other. The automatic management reduces the complexity traditionally associated with certificate handling.

Managing Certificates and Identity

Verify the Identity Service

Ensure that the Identity service is running correctly in both clusters.

You can check the service's status and logs using:

```
kubectl -n linkerd get po -l linkerd.io/control-plane-component=identity
kubectl -n linkerd logs -l linkerd.io/control-plane-component=identity
```

Rotate Certificates

While Linkerd automatically rotates the proxies' certificates, you might need to manually rotate the trust root certificate, which is the root of trust for the entire mesh.

Generate a new trust root and issuer certificates. Use the step tool or similar to generate these certificates.

Use the Linkerd CLI to rotate the trust root:

```
linkerd upgrade --identity-trust-anchors-file=/path/to/new-trust-root.crt --
identity-issuer-certificate-file=/path/to/new-issuer.crt --identity-issuer-key-
file=/path/to/new-issuer.key | kubectl apply -f -
```

Automate Certificate Renewal
Ensure that the automatic renewal of certificates by the Identity service is functioning as expected.

You can monitor the expiry of certificates using the Linkerd dashboard or through logs. This ensures that certificates are being rotated before they expire.

Integrating with External Certificate Authorities
If FusionCorp has an existing certificate authority (CA), they might want to integrate it with Linkerd.

Linkerd supports integration with external CAs. This process involves configuring Linkerd to use the external CA for issuing certificates.

You may also refer to Linkerd's documentation for specific steps to integrate with external CAs like HashiCorp Vault or cert-manager.

Identity Control and Verification
Ensure that the identities assigned to each service are appropriate and verify the authenticity of these identities.

Regularly validate that the identities assigned to services match their intended roles and responsibilities within the mesh.

Use Linkerd's CLI or dashboard to inspect the identities.

Authorization Policy and Its Implementation

Understanding Linkerd's Authorization Policy

Linkerd's authorization policy provides fine-grained control over the types of communication that can reach meshed pods, which is an important part of building a zero-trust security paradigm in a Kubernetes context. Linkerd's authorization policy works on the principle of denying access to resources unless certain conditions are met. This is based on the TLS identity of the client or the source IP address.

The policy is configured using two mechanisms:

51

1. Default Policies: Set at cluster, namespace, workload, or pod level through Kubernetes annotations.
2. Custom Resource Definitions (CRDs): Specify fine-grained policy for specific ports, routes, workloads, etc.

Implementing Authorization Policy

Setting Cluster-Wide Default Policy

Initially, set a cluster-wide default policy. For a strict zero-trust model, start with a deny policy:

```
kubectl annotate namespace default config.linkerd.io/default-inbound-
policy=deny
```

This will prohibit any traffic to any meshed pod in the default namespace, requiring explicit allowance through CRDs.

Defining Fine-Grained Policies with CRDs

A Server CRD defines traffic targets (like a port) for a set of pods within a namespace. For instance, FusionCorp might define a server for backend services in Cluster-Beta:

```
apiVersion: policy.linkerd.io/v1beta1
kind: Server
metadata:
  name: backend-svc
spec:
  podSelector:
    matchLabels:
      app: backend
  port: 8080
  proxyProtocol: HTTP/2
```

MeshTLSAuthentication and NetworkAuthentication CRDs define what qualifies as valid authentication.

For example, Allow traffic only from certain namespaces or with specific identities:

```
apiVersion: policy.linkerd.io/v1beta1
kind: MeshTLSAuthentication
metadata:
  name: authenticated-clients
spec:
  networks: []
  identities:
    - "frontend.cluster-alpha.svc.cluster.local"
```

AuthorizationPolicy CRDs map the authentication rules to the targets. For example, allow traffic to backend-svc only if it matches authenticated-clients:

```
apiVersion: policy.linkerd.io/v1beta1
kind: AuthorizationPolicy
metadata:
  name: allow-authenticated-frontend
spec:
  targetRef:
    kind: Server
    name: backend-svc
  requiredAuthenticationRefs:
    - kind: MeshTLSAuthentication
      name: authenticated-clients
```

Customizing Policies for Specific Services

Suppose FusionCorp has a service payment-service in Cluster-Beta that should only be accessed by certain clients.

First, create a Server for payment-service:

```
apiVersion: policy.linkerd.io/v1beta1
```

```
kind: Server
metadata:
  name: payment-svc
  namespace: finance
spec:
  podSelector:
    matchLabels:
      app: payment-service
  port: 443
  proxyProtocol: HTTPS
```

This defines a server on port 443 for pods labeled app: payment-service in the finance namespace.

Next, define a ServerAuthorization to restrict access to this server:

```
apiVersion: policy.linkerd.io/v1beta1
kind: ServerAuthorization
metadata:
  name: payment-svc-auth
  namespace: finance
spec:
  server:
    name: payment-svc
  client:
    meshTLS:
      identities:
        - "frontend.cluster-alpha.svc.cluster.local"
        - "audit.cluster-alpha.svc.cluster.local"
```

This policy allows only clients with specific TLS identities (frontend and audit services from Cluster-Alpha) to access payment-service.

Apply these configurations to the Cluster-Beta:

```
kubectl apply -f payment-svc.yaml
kubectl apply -f payment-svc-auth.yaml
```

Ensure the policies are correctly applied and functioning as expected:

Check logs or use Linkerd's dashboard to verify that only authorized traffic reaches payment-service.

Test access from unauthorized clients to ensure they are correctly denied.

With this implementation, FusionCorp can effectively manage who can access what within their service mesh, ensuring compliance with their stringent security requirements.

End-to-End Traffic Security

When working with Kubernetes and Linkerd in particular, it is important to secure end-to-end traffic by encrypting and authenticating all communication routes between the request initiator and the receiver. Securing end-to-end traffic is of utmost importance to FusionCorp in order to safeguard sensitive data and ensure the continued integrity of their services in both Cluster-Alpha and Cluster-Beta.

To accomplish this with Linkerd, follow these steps:

Enforce Automated mTLS

Linkerd automatically enables mTLS for all meshed services. This encrypts and authenticates traffic between services.

To ensure mTLS is active, you can check the tap output or Linkerd dashboard. For example:

```
linkerd -n finance tap deploy/payment-service
```

This command shows live traffic for payment-service, including mTLS details.

Secure Ingress and Egress Traffic

Ingress Configuration

Secure ingress traffic (traffic entering the cluster) by integrating Linkerd with your ingress controller (e.g., Nginx, Traefik).

Ensure the ingress controller is part of the Linkerd mesh. This involves injecting the Linkerd proxy into the ingress controller pods.

For example, the command to inject Linkerd into an Nginx ingress controller:

```
kubectl get deploy nginx-ingress-controller -n nginx -o yaml | linkerd inject - |
kubectl apply -f -
```

Egress Configuration

For securing egress traffic (traffic leaving the cluster), use Linkerd's ServiceEntry resource.

Define external services that your cluster needs to communicate with and apply mTLS to this traffic.

For example, ServiceEntry for an external database:

```
apiVersion: networking.istio.io/v1alpha3
kind: ServiceEntry
metadata:
  name: external-db
spec:
  hosts:
  - db.example.com
  ports:
  - number: 5432
    name: tcp
    protocol: TCP
  location: MESH_EXTERNAL
```

Kubernetes Network Policies

Enhance security by defining Kubernetes network policies that restrict which pods can communicate with each other.

Example policy to allow traffic only from specific namespaces or pods:

```yaml
apiVersion: networking.k8s.io/v1
kind: NetworkPolicy
metadata:
  name: allow-frontend
  namespace: finance
spec:
  podSelector:
    matchLabels:
      app: payment-service
  ingress:
  - from:
    - podSelector:
        matchLabels:
          app: frontend
```

Define Service Profiles

Create Linkerd service profiles to specify per-route policies for retries, timeouts, and response classes.

This granular control can enhance security by limiting retries or defining custom conditions for route failures.

An example of a service profile:

```yaml
apiVersion: linkerd.io/v1alpha2
kind: ServiceProfile
```

```yaml
metadata:
  name: payment-service.finance.svc.cluster.local
spec:
  routes:
  - name: payment-retry-route
    condition:
      method: POST
      pathRegex: /api/v1/payments
    isRetryable: true
```

Summary

In this chapter, we examined Linkerd as the central mechanism for interservice security in a Kubernetes system. We started by studying interservice security, which includes the four main features of safe communication in a microservices architecture: authentication, authorization, encryption, and data integrity. The chapter emphasized the importance of fundamental security concepts in distributed systems, particularly given the dynamic and complicated nature of Kubernetes deployments. It was determined that a comprehensive approach to security is required, which includes not just technological solutions but also adherence to best security standards.

We looked into the mechanics of how Linkerd implemented automatic mutual TLS (mTLS). This feature is critical for communication security since it ensures encryption and mutual authentication between services. The practical methods for configuring and verifying mTLS in FusionCorp's multi-cluster architecture were described, with an emphasis on its ease of automation and integration. Following that, we concentrated on creating and customizing authorization policies with Linkerd. This included establishing default rules and leveraging Custom Resource Definitions (CRDs) to provide fine-grained access control for individual services, such as FusionCorp's payment service. The approach emphasized the significance of setting clear and exact access rules that are aligned with the specific operational and security requirements of various services.

The chapter also addressed the vital challenge of securing end-to-end traffic, which is required for data protection in transit across the service mesh. We reviewed the detailed methods for securing both entrance and egress traffic, implementing network policies for additional security layers, and using service profiles for per-route policies. This solution ensures that all traffic within

FusionCorp's clusters is properly encrypted, monitored, and controlled. The main takeaway from this chapter is that protecting communications in a Kubernetes context, especially with a service mesh like Linkerd, necessitates a comprehensive approach. This strategy combines technological solutions with security best practices to enable robust, dependable, and compliant interservice connections.

CHAPTER 5: ADVANCED TRAFFIC MANAGEMENT

Introduction to Traffic Management

Brief Overview

In traditional monolithic architectures, traffic management is relatively straightforward due to the centralized nature of the application. Standard load balancing, simple round-robin algorithms, and basic failover strategies often suffice. However, the advent of microservices has dramatically changed the landscape. Microservices are inherently distributed and dynamic, with services frequently scaling up or down and instances being ephematically created and destroyed. This dynamism makes it challenging to keep track of service instances and their health using standard methods. Unlike monolithic applications, microservices often have complex interdependencies. Traffic needs to be routed and managed not just to the services but often through a chain of services, which requires sophisticated routing logic.

Standard load balancers cannot understand the nuances of application-level requirements. Microservices might need traffic management based on HTTP headers, cookies, or other application-level information, which standard tools are not equipped to handle.

Ensuring high availability and resilience in a distributed system is more challenging. Standard approaches may not effectively handle scenarios like cascading failures, where the failure of one service impacts others. Microservices can exhibit highly variable traffic patterns, necessitating more adaptive and responsive traffic management solutions.

Necessity for Advanced Traffic Management

To address these challenges, advanced traffic management strategies become essential:
- Intelligent Load Balancing: Beyond simple round-robin or IP-hash algorithms, intelligent load balancing can distribute traffic based on current load, response times, or even specific content within the requests.
- Canary Deployments and A/B Testing: These techniques involve routing a subset of traffic to new service versions for testing purposes. They are crucial for continuous deployment environments but require sophisticated traffic routing capabilities.
- Circuit Breakers and Bulkheads: In a microservices architecture, it's vital to isolate failures and prevent them from cascading. Circuit breakers stop traffic to failing services, while bulkheads isolate services to prevent failures from spreading.
- Rate Limiting and Throttling: To manage the load on services and prevent overloading, rate limiting and throttling are necessary. These measures control the amount of traffic a service receives over a given period.
- Timeouts and Retries: Properly configuring timeouts and retries ensures that the system can gracefully handle transient failures, which are common in distributed systems.
- Service Mesh as a Solution: Service meshes like Linkerd offer a comprehensive solution for advanced traffic management. They provide fine-grained control, allowing operators

to direct, control, and monitor traffic in a way that traditional tools cannot.

- Observability and Monitoring: Advanced traffic management requires extensive monitoring and observability to understand traffic patterns, identify bottlenecks, and troubleshoot issues. Service meshes typically come integrated with powerful monitoring tools.

Prospects of Advanced Traffic Management

Several critical steps are involved in FusionCorp's strategic effort to adopt advanced traffic management. First, they're integrating Linkerd into their system. This deployment is critical for managing traffic throughout their microservices architecture, as it enables advanced capabilities such as intelligent load balancing, secure communication, and traffic splitting. They are using Linkerd's traffic splitting features to implement canary installations. This enables them to route a part of traffic to fresh service versions for testing.

In addition, FusionCorp is working on introducing resilience patterns within Linkerd. This includes installing circuit breakers and bulkheads, which are essential for isolating and managing service outages. Another crucial aspect is defining rate limits and throttles, especially for services that may experience huge traffic spikes, to ensure their stability and responsiveness.

Finally, they are harnessing the power of observability. FusionCorp obtains real-time insights into traffic flows and performance data using Linkerd's dashboard and Prometheus connection. This complete approach to advanced traffic management enables FusionCorp to successfully manage the changing needs of their service landscape.

Organize Services and Traffic Routes

We will explore practical methods for organizing service interactions and routing strategies in FusionCorp's current Linkerd architecture so that traffic paths may be properly managed. FusionCorp's microservices design, which spans Cluster-Alpha and Cluster-Beta, necessitates precise management to ensure peak performance and reliability.

Given below is how this can be done with Linkerd:

Define Service Boundaries Clearly

Services should be organized based on their functional boundaries. For instance, FusionCorp's Cluster-Alpha handles frontend services, while Cluster-Beta manages backend services like databases and analytics. This separation aids in managing traffic flows logically and ensuring that services are scalable and maintainable.

Service Discovery and Routing

Use Linkerd's service discovery capabilities to dynamically route traffic to the appropriate instances of a service. Linkerd automatically updates the routing as services scale up or down, ensuring that traffic is always directed to the right destination.

Implement Traffic Splits for Canary Deployments

Suppose FusionCorp wants to roll out a new version of a frontend service in Cluster-Alpha. They can use Linkerd's TrafficSplit resource to direct a portion of the traffic to the new version.

A TrafficSplit might look like this:

```
apiVersion: split.smi-spec.io/v1alpha1
kind: TrafficSplit
metadata:
  name: frontend-split
  namespace: default
spec:
  service: frontend-svc
  backends:
  - service: frontend-svc-v1
    weight: 500m
  - service: frontend-svc-v2
    weight: 500m
```

This configuration splits traffic evenly between frontend-svc-v1 (the existing version) and frontend-svc-v2 (the new version).

For more granular control, FusionCorp can manage traffic at the route level within a service. They can define ServiceProfiles in Linkerd to specify routes within a service and apply specific rules or weights to those routes.

A ServiceProfile might look like this:

```
apiVersion: linkerd.io/v1alpha2
```

```
kind: ServiceProfile
metadata:
  name: frontend-svc.default.svc.cluster.local
  namespace: default
spec:
  routes:
  - name: new-feature
    condition:
      pathRegex: /api/new-feature
    weight: 0.1
  - name: all-other
    condition:
      not:
        pathRegex: /api/new-feature
    weight: 0.9
```

This directs most traffic to existing routes while routing a smaller portion to a new feature path.

Override Error Codes

Overriding error codes is particularly important in microservices architectures where you have a multitude of services interacting with each other, often over a network. By managing error codes effectively, FusionCorp can fine-tune the behavior of their services in response to various error conditions, enhancing both the user experience and system resilience.

Understanding Concept

In a microservices environment, services communicate via network calls, which can fail for various reasons (network issues, service unavailability, etc.). These failures are typically indicated by HTTP error codes, like 404 (Not Found), 503 (Service Unavailable), etc. Standard error handling might not always be optimal in a distributed system, as it may not consider the specific context or interdependencies of the services.

Purpose of Overriding Error Codes

Overriding error codes allows you to define custom responses or behaviors for specific error conditions. This can be used to implement more sophisticated error handling strategies than what is provided by default.

For instance, a service might retry a request if it receives a 503 error, or it might redirect to a fallback service if it gets a 404 error.

Situations for Overriding Error Codes

- Network glitches or temporary issues in a service can cause transient errors. Custom error handling can implement retries or backoff strategies.
- If a service depends on another service that is failing, overriding error codes can redirect traffic or implement fallback logic.
- During high traffic, some services might return errors due to overloading. Custom responses can help in gracefully degrading the service.
- During deployments or upgrades, services might temporarily be unavailable. Custom error handling can ensure smoother transitions and maintain availability.

Linkerd Facilitates Error Code Overriding

Linkerd provides mechanisms to customize how services within its mesh handle different types of errors. This is achieved through:

Service Profiles

Service Profiles in Linkerd allow you to define custom routes within a service, along with specific rules for handling errors for each route. You can specify retries, timeouts, and failure conditions on a per-route basis.

Retry and Timeout Policies

By defining retry and timeout policies in Service Profiles, you can control how services respond to specific error codes. For example, you can configure a service to retry on receiving a 503 error but fail immediately on a 401 (Unauthorized) error.

In the next section, we will practically apply these concepts to FusionCorp's environment, demonstrating how to customize the handling of error codes for their services using Linkerd.

Sample Program: Overriding Error Codes

Building on what we have learned so far, we should put FusionCorp's ability to bypass error codes via Linkerd's Service Profiles to the test. Their applications' overall robustness and user experience are improved with this functionality, which allows for more precise control over how services in

Cluster-Alpha and Cluster-Beta respond to specific problems.

Think about an external API called by FusionCorp's customer-service in Cluster-Alpha. Due to temporary issues, this external API occasionally returns a 503 Service Unavailable response. FusionCorp is planning to introduce a new policy that will automatically retry requests when a 503 error occurs, but will not do so when other error codes, such as 404 Not Found or 401 Unauthorized, are encountered.

Create Service Profile

Generate a Basic Service Profile

First, if a Service Profile doesn't already exist for customer-service, generate a basic one using Linkerd's CLI:

```
linkerd profile --namespace default --open-api customer-service.swagger.yaml
customer-service > customer-service-profile.yaml
```

This command assumes that FusionCorp has an OpenAPI (Swagger) specification for customer-service. If not, they can create a Service Profile manually.

Modify the Service Profile to Add Retries

Edit customer-service-profile.yaml to include retry logic for 503 errors:

```
apiVersion: linkerd.io/v1alpha2
kind: ServiceProfile
metadata:
  name: customer-service.default.svc.cluster.local
  namespace: default
spec:
  routes:
    - name: retry-on-503
      condition:
        method: GET
        pathRegex: /api/v1/data
      isRetryable: true
```

```
      timeout: 10s
      responseClasses:
        - condition:
            status:
              min: 503
              max: 503
          isFailure: false
```

This Service Profile defines a route for GET requests to /api/v1/data. It marks 503 as a retriable status and sets a timeout of 10 seconds for the retry.

Apply the Service Profile

Deploy the Service Profile

Apply the modified Service Profile to Cluster-Alpha:

```
kubectl apply -f customer-service-profile.yaml
```

Check the Service Profile

Ensure the Service Profile is correctly applied to customer-service:

```
linkerd -n default routes svc/customer-service --profile
```

This command shows the routes defined in the Service Profile for customer-service.

Monitor Behavior

Observe the behavior of customer-service using Linkerd's dashboard or logs. Confirm that the service now retries on encountering a 503 error, improving its resilience to temporary external API downtimes.

An impressive feature of Linkerd's Service Profiles is the ability to provide retry logic for certain error circumstances, such as 503 Service Unavailable, without impacting the processing of other problems. Thanks to this feature, FusionCorp can modify its microservices' behavior to handle external dependencies and unexpected scenarios with grace.

Timeouts in Action

Timeouts prevent services from waiting indefinitely for responses from other services, which is crucial in a distributed environment like FusionCorp's.

Understanding Timeouts in Linkerd

Timeouts in Linkerd are configured at the route level within Service Profiles. They define the maximum duration a proxy should wait for a response from a service before considering the request failed. This mechanism helps in handling scenarios where a service might be down or slow to respond, preventing cascading failures and ensuring better system resilience.

We shall explore how FusionCorp can implement timeouts using Linkerd's Service Profiles in their Cluster-Alpha and Cluster-Beta.

Sample Program: Implementing Timeouts Strategy

Assume FusionCorp has a reporting-service in Cluster-Beta, which occasionally experiences slow response times due to heavy data processing. To prevent these delays from impacting the overall user experience, FusionCorp decides to implement a timeout strategy.

Create or Modify a Service Profile

If a Service Profile doesn't exist for reporting-service, create one. If it exists, modify it to include a timeout:

```
apiVersion: linkerd.io/v1alpha2
kind: ServiceProfile
metadata:
  name: reporting-service.default.svc.cluster.local
  namespace: default
spec:
  routes:
    - name: report-generation
      condition:
        method: POST
        pathRegex: /api/v1/generateReport
```

```
timeout: 20s
```

This Service Profile specifies a 20-second timeout for POST requests to the /api/v1/generateReport endpoint.

Deploy the Service Profile
Apply this configuration to Cluster-Beta:

```
kubectl apply -f reporting-service-profile.yaml
```

Check the Service Profile
Verify that the Service Profile is applied correctly:

```
linkerd -n default routes svc/reporting-service --profile
```

This command displays the routes and their configurations for reporting-service.

Observe the Service Behavior
Use the Linkerd dashboard or logs to monitor reporting-service.

Look for instances where the service takes longer than 20 seconds to respond, and ensure that the timeout is correctly triggered.

Fine-Tuning
Based on monitoring data, FusionCorp may need to adjust the timeout duration. For instance, if the 20-second timeout is too short for most report generation tasks, it can be increased.

Update the Service Profile to change the timeout value and reapply it.

Best Practices for Managing Timeouts

- Set timeouts that balance the need for quick responses with the operational realities of the service. Too short timeouts can lead to unnecessary retries, while too long timeouts can delay failure recovery.
- Regularly monitor the impact of timeouts and be ready to iterate on the configurations as the behavior of your services evolves.
- In some cases, combining timeouts with retry policies can provide a more resilient solution. However, this should be done carefully to avoid overwhelming services with retry traffic.

By setting appropriate timeouts and regularly monitoring their impact, FusionCorp can ensure that their services remain responsive and performant, even in the face of potential delays or issues in the service processing.

Load Balancing and Its Techniques

Linkerd provides sophisticated load balancing capabilities that are critical for efficiently distributing traffic across services in a microservices architecture like FusionCorp's. These capabilities are designed to optimize response times and resource utilization, thereby enhancing the overall performance and reliability of the application.

How Linkerd Facilitates Load Balancing?

Linkerd implements advanced load balancing at the proxy level, ensuring that traffic is distributed effectively across available service instances.

Dynamic Load Balancing

Linkerd's proxies automatically perform load balancing for each outbound request. Unlike traditional load balancers that might use simple algorithms like round-robin, Linkerd's load balancing is dynamic and adaptive. It considers factors such as request success rates, latencies, and the number of in-flight requests, allowing for more intelligent traffic distribution.

Latency-Aware Load Balancing

Linkerd proxies continuously monitor and record the latency of requests to each instance of a service. This information is used to make informed load balancing decisions, prioritizing instances with lower response times. This approach helps in avoiding overloading slower instances and improves the overall responsiveness of the application.

Load Balancer Types

Linkerd supports various types of load balancers, like EWMA (Exponentially Weighted Moving Average), which is latency-aware, and least-request, which considers the number of in-flight requests.

Sample Program: Using Load Balancing Technique

Consider that FusionCorp's customer-analytics service in Cluster-Alpha experiences varying loads throughout the day. To optimize traffic distribution to this service, different load balancing strategies will be implemented.

Implementing Latency-Aware Load Balancing

By default, Linkerd's proxies use a latency-aware load balancing algorithm (EWMA). FusionCorp can ensure this feature is enabled for optimal performance during varying load conditions. Monitor the customer-analytics service using Linkerd's dashboard to observe how traffic is distributed based on instance latencies.

Least-Request Load Balancing

Although Linkerd doesn't natively support least-request load balancing, FusionCorp can experiment with a similar strategy by adjusting the number of replicas for customer-analytics based on in-flight requests. Use Kubernetes Horizontal Pod Autoscaler (HPA) to scale the customer-analytics service based on the number of in-flight requests.

Deploy HPA

Apply an HPA configuration that scales the number of pods based on current request load:

```yaml
apiVersion: autoscaling/v2beta2
kind: HorizontalPodAutoscaler
metadata:
  name: customer-analytics-hpa
  namespace: default
spec:
  scaleTargetRef:
    apiVersion: apps/v1
    kind: Deployment
    name: customer-analytics
  minReplicas: 1
  maxReplicas: 10
  metrics:
  - type: Resource
    resource:
      name: requests
      target:
        type: Utilization
```

This HPA configuration increases the number of customer-analytics pods when the number of in-flight requests is high.

Monitor and Adjust

Use the Linkerd dashboard to monitor the effect of these load balancing strategies on the customer-analytics service. Pay attention to metrics like response times, success rates, and request volumes. Based on the observed data, FusionCorp might need to adjust the load balancing strategies, such as changing the HPA thresholds or tuning the proxy configurations.

Integrating Kubernetes functionalities like HPA and utilizing features like latency-aware load balancing allow FusionCorp to react to changing traffic patterns while maintaining excellent service performance and reliability.

Canary Deployments

Definition

Canary deployments are a method used in software development to roll out changes to a small subset of users before making them available to everybody. This technique reduces the risk of introducing a new software version in production by gradually increasing its exposure and monitoring its performance and behavior.

Linkerd supports canary deployments through its traffic splitting feature, which allows you to divide traffic between different versions of a service. Linkerd uses the SMI (Service Mesh Interface) TrafficSplit resource to control how traffic is sent to different versions of a service.

Following are the components of TrafficSplit:
- Service (root): The Kubernetes service that traffic is sent to.
- Backends: The different versions of the service (e.g., current and new versions) along with the proportion of traffic that each should receive.

Features

- Gradual Rollout: Canary deployments involve releasing a new version of a service to a limited number of users initially. If this version performs well and doesn't introduce any regressions, it can then be rolled out to the rest of the users.

- Risk Mitigation: This approach helps identify any issues with the new release under real usage conditions but with minimal impact.

- Feedback-Driven: Real-time feedback from the canary version is used to decide whether to proceed with the rollout, roll back, or fix issues that were detected.

Sample Program: Implementing Canary Deployments

Assuming that FusionCorp wants to test a new version (v2) of their product-catalog service in Cluster-Alpha.

Deploy the New Version

Deploy product-catalog-v2 alongside the existing product-catalog (v1) in Cluster-Alpha. And, ensure both versions are running and meshed with Linkerd.

Define TrafficSplit

Create a TrafficSplit object to split traffic between v1 and v2.

```
apiVersion: split.smi-spec.io/v1alpha2
kind: TrafficSplit
metadata:
  name: product-catalog-rollout
  namespace: default
spec:
  service: product-catalog
  backends:
    - service: product-catalog-v1
      weight: 900m
    - service: product-catalog-v2
      weight: 100m
```

This configuration directs 10% of the traffic to v2 and the rest to v1.

Deploy TrafficSplit

Apply the TrafficSplit configuration:

```
kubectl apply -f traffic-split-product-catalog.yaml
```

Use Linkerd's dashboard to monitor product-catalog-v2. Look for errors, increased latency, or any other issues.

If v2 performs well, gradually increase its traffic weight in the TrafficSplit resource and decrease the weight for v1.

If issues arise, reduce the weight for v2 or roll back entirely.

Full Rollout or Rollback
Once confident, shift 100% of the traffic to v2. In case of critical issues, revert to v1 by adjusting the weights in the TrafficSplit resource.

Using the TrafficSplit resource, users can manage the flow of traffic between different service versions. This lets them roll out upgrades incrementally, see how they affect things, and use real-world data to decide whether to roll back or roll out completely. The dangers of delivering new software versions are greatly reduced by this strategy.

Implement A/B Testing

Understanding A/B Testing

A/B Testing in the context of software development and operations refers to a methodology where two or more versions of a component (like a web page, service endpoint, etc.) are compared in terms of performance and effectiveness. This comparison is done in a controlled environment with real users and provides valuable insights into which version performs better based on defined metrics.

A/B testing involves splitting traffic between different versions of a service or application feature to compare their performance. Each variant is shown to a different segment of users, and data is collected on how each performs. The goal is to make informed decisions based on user response data. Metrics could include user engagement, conversion rates, error rates, or any other relevant performance indicator. Unlike synthetic tests or staged rollouts, A/B testing provides feedback from real user interactions, offering more authentic insights.

Sample Program: A/B Testing with Linkerd

For A/B testing, you can use Linkerd's traffic split feature. Splitting the traffic across several service versions allows you to see how they change the user experience or the overall performance of the system.

For example, imagine that FusionCorp is interested in using Cluster-Alpha to evaluate a potential update to its user-interface-service. User-interface-service-featureA and user-interface-service-featureB are the two versions that they have created.

Prepare Variants

Ensure both variants of the user-interface-service are deployed in Cluster-Alpha. Both variants should be running simultaneously and be meshed with Linkerd.

Define TrafficSplit

Create a TrafficSplit object to distribute traffic between the two variants.

```
apiVersion: split.smi-spec.io/v1alpha2
kind: TrafficSplit
metadata:
  name: ui-service-ab-test
  namespace: default
spec:
  service: user-interface-service
  backends:
    - service: user-interface-service-featureA
      weight: 500m
    - service: user-interface-service-featureB
      weight: 500m
```

This directs 50% of the traffic to each variant.

Deploy TrafficSplit

Apply the configuration to Cluster-Alpha:

```
kubectl apply -f traffic-split-ui-service.yaml
```

Observe User Interaction and System Metrics:

Monitor both variants using Linkerd's dashboard. Collect data on user engagement, response times, error rates, or other relevant metrics. Optionally, use additional analytics tools to gather user feedback or engagement metrics.

Evaluate Performance

Compare the performance of featureA and featureB. Determine which variant meets the objectives more effectively based on the collected data.

Based on the analysis, decide which feature to implement fully. Adjust the TrafficSplit weights to shift all traffic to the chosen variant or roll back to the original version if neither performs adequately.

This approach ensures that any changes to the services are backed by concrete data, reducing the risks associated with new feature rollouts.

Handling Peak Loads

When the system is experiencing peak loads, it is essential to properly manage traffic in order to keep the system's performance and availability as high as possible. There are a number of capabilities that Linkerd provides that can assist FusionCorp in effectively managing situations like these. The strategy entails making use of Linkerd's capabilities in order to dynamically adjust to the increased network traffic and guarantee that the services will continue to be resilient.

Peak Load Management Approaches

Real-Time Traffic Monitoring

Continuously monitor traffic patterns using Linkerd's dashboard. This real-time data helps in identifying services that are experiencing high traffic volumes.

Load Balancing Adjustments

Rely on Linkerd's dynamic load balancing, which automatically adjusts to the changing traffic and distributes it across available service instances. This feature ensures no single instance is overwhelmed.

Autoscaling Services

Utilize Kubernetes Horizontal Pod Autoscaler (HPA) in conjunction with Linkerd. While Linkerd itself doesn't directly scale services, it works seamlessly with Kubernetes' scaling features. Configure HPA for critical services that are likely to experience traffic spikes, so they automatically scale based on predefined metrics like CPU usage or request volume.

Sample Program: Managing Peak Loads

Suppose FusionCorp is expecting its order-processing service to see a peak load while they are in Cluster-Beta.

Setup HPA for order-processing

If not already configured, set up HPA for the order-processing service to handle increased load. Example of an HPA configuration:

```
apiVersion: autoscaling/v2beta2
kind: HorizontalPodAutoscaler
metadata:
  name: order-processing-hpa
  namespace: default
spec:
  scaleTargetRef:
    apiVersion: apps/v1
    kind: Deployment
    name: order-processing
  minReplicas: 3
  maxReplicas: 15
  metrics:
  - type: Resource
    resource:
      name: cpu
      target:
        type: Utilization
        averageUtilization: 75
```

This HPA scales the number of pods for order-processing based on CPU utilization, maintaining efficient handling of incoming requests.

Use Linkerd Dashboard

Continuously monitor the order-processing service through Linkerd's dashboard during the peak load period. Pay attention to metrics like request volume, success rates, and response times.

Fine-Tune Load Balancing

Based on the observed data, consider adjusting load balancing parameters if certain pods are consistently under more strain. This could involve tweaking the load balancer settings within Linkerd's proxy configuration, though often Linkerd's default settings are sufficient for dynamic adjustments.

Update HPA Settings

Modify the HPA settings for order-processing if the scaling does not align well with the load patterns. Adjust the minReplicas, maxReplicas, or averageUtilization values to better accommodate the observed traffic demands.

Implement Rate Limiting

In cases where services are at risk of being overwhelmed, consider implementing rate limiting. Rate limiting can be configured in the Linkerd proxy to limit the number of requests a service can receive in a given time frame.

A combination of real-time monitoring, dynamic load balancing, autoscaling services with HPA, and possibly implementing rate limiting are required in order to handle peak loads in the environment that FusionCorp uses with Linkerd.

Integrations with Tools

An increase in the overall functionality and efficiency of the service mesh is achieved through the integration of Linkerd with other tools such as Jenkins, Prometheus, Jaeger, and Amazon Web Services (AWS). This provides users with a significant amount of value, particularly in an environment as complex as FusionCorp's. The advantages of these integrations will be learned, and we will show you how to put them into practice in the real world.

Integration with Jenkins

Service deployments are made easier and more automated with the integration of Jenkins and Linkerd in FusionCorp's Kubernetes environment. In this configuration, Jenkins is set up to automate deployments and works in tandem with Linkerd to ensure that service version updates go smoothly. As a whole, the development process is improved by this integration, which boosts the continuous delivery pipeline. Setting up a Jenkins pipeline to automatically inject Linkerd proxies into Kubernetes deployments is the practical aspect to consider. Automated and efficient deployment management is achieved through a scripted pipeline process that reads the deployment configurations from Kubernetes, integrates Linkerd, and applies the changes to the cluster.

Below is the script to successfully integrate:

```
pipeline {
    agent any
    stages {
        stage('Deploy') {
            steps {
                script {
                    def kubeConfig = loadKubeConfig()
                    def deployYaml = readFile(file: 'k8s-deploy.yaml')
                    def linkerdYaml = sh(script: "echo '${deployYaml}' | linkerd inject -", returnStdout: true)
                    sh "echo '${linkerdYaml}' | kubectl apply -f -"
                }
            }
        }
    }
}
```

This script reads a Kubernetes deployment YAML, injects Linkerd, and applies it to the cluster.

Integration with Prometheus

Service monitoring capabilities are greatly improved by integrating Prometheus with Linkerd at FusionCorp. The combined results provide a comprehensive picture of the state and efficiency of the service. In order to conduct in-depth performance analysis, FusionCorp relies on Prometheus's integration to monitor unique metrics that are designed to meet their unique service requirements. Implementing this solution in practice entails setting up Prometheus to efficiently scrape metrics made available by Linkerd. Prometheus is configured to properly monitor and report on metrics from Linkerd proxies within the Kubernetes environment.

Following is the script to integrate prometheus with our linkerd setup::

```
scrape_configs:
 - job_name: 'linkerd'
   kubernetes_sd_configs:
   - role: pod
   relabel_configs:
   - source_labels: [__meta_kubernetes_pod_container_name]
     action: keep
     regex: ^linkerd-proxy$
   - source_labels: [__meta_kubernetes_namespace]
     target_label: namespace
   - source_labels: [__meta_kubernetes_pod_name]
     target_label: pod
```

This setup is accomplished by defining specific scrape configurations in Prometheus. If you want to know how your Linkerd-managed services are doing in terms of operation at any given moment, this setup is crucial.

Integration with Jaeger

The capacity to perform distributed tracing is improved by integrating Jaeger into FusionCorp's setup. Requests across various services can be tracked and visualized in great detail with Jaeger's capabilities. Identifying performance issues like bottlenecks and latency is where this really shines.

In order to put this into action, Jaeger is set up inside the Kubernetes cluster as below:

```
apiVersion: linkerd.io/v1alpha2
kind: LinkerdConfig
metadata:
  name: linkerd-config
spec:
```

```
proxy:
  tracing:
    enabled: true
    collectorSvcAddr: jaeger-collector.jaeger.svc.cluster.local:14268
```

Performance optimization and service monitoring are both greatly aided by having detailed tracing information captured and made available for analysis after Linkerd is set up to send trace data to Jaeger.

These integrations streamline the deployment processes, provide deeper insights into service performance, enable effective tracing of service requests, and utilize cloud resources efficiently. For FusionCorp, this translates to increased agility, better observability, improved operational efficiency, and robust service management in their cloud-native ecosystem.

Summary

This chapter explored advanced approaches to traffic management in FusionCorp's microservices architecture, with an emphasis on the challenges and requirements of contemporary cloud-native apps. As a first step, we highlighted the need for advanced techniques in a distributed and dynamic service landscape by addressing the limitations of standard traffic management. This chapter demonstrated how conventional approaches fail miserably when faced with microservices' complex interdependencies, heterogeneous traffic patterns, and resilience demands. To guarantee high availability and optimal service performance, it was stressed that intelligent load balancing, adaptive traffic routing, and the implementation of strong failover strategies were crucial.

We continued our exploration by demonstrating how to use Linkerd in FusionCorp's setup for advanced traffic management techniques. Strategies such as latency-aware routing and using Kubernetes features like Horizontal Pod Autoscaler to approximate least-request load balancing were covered in detail, along with how to use Linkerd for effective load balancing. Using Linkerd's traffic splitting capabilities, we demonstrated how to conduct A/B testing, which compares two or more service versions in real-world user scenarios. In addition, the chapter covered how to deal with peak load situations, stressing the significance of autoscaling, dynamic load balancing adjustments, and real-time traffic monitoring to keep services stable and performant during peak traffic times. Finally, we investigated how Linkerd could be integrated with other important tools, such as Jenkins for automated deployments, Prometheus for improved monitoring, Jaeger for distributed tracing. The integrations were covered in depth, showing how these synergies improve observability, control over FusionCorp's microservices infrastructure, and efficiency.

Overall, FusionCorp was prepared to handle the difficulties of traffic management in a complicated service mesh environment thanks to the information and resources provided in Chapter 5. When it comes to monitoring and managing their services, FusionCorp can make sure they are resilient and responsive under different loads and conditions by using Linkerd's advanced features and integrations.

CHAPTER 6: MULTI-CLUSTER COMMUNICATION AND ROLLOUTS

Fundamentals of Multi-Cluster Communication

Organizations frequently encounter the challenge of overseeing numerous Kubernetes clusters in the modern era's vast and varied IT environments. Many requirements can lead to a multi-cluster configuration, including but not limited to: geographical distribution, concern separation, data residency law compliance, or simply outgrowing the capabilities of a single cluster.

Necessity of Multi-Cluster Communication

Multi-cluster communication enables different clusters to share data and services seamlessly. It allows FusionCorp to optimize resource utilization by distributing workloads across clusters, leading to improved performance and efficiency. For example, a user-facing application in one cluster might need to access a payment processing service in another, necessitating secure and reliable inter-cluster communication.

Moreover, multi-cluster setups can enhance disaster recovery strategies. By spreading resources across multiple clusters, organizations can avoid single points of failure, ensuring higher availability and resilience. In FusionCorp's case, if one cluster faces an outage, other clusters can take over, minimizing service disruption.

What is Multi-Cluster Communication?

Multi-cluster communication refers to the ability of services running in separate Kubernetes clusters to discover and interact with each other as if they were part of a single cluster. This communication is pivotal for FusionCorp to maintain consistency and continuity of operations across their international infrastructure. It involves complex networking, security, and service discovery mechanisms to ensure seamless integration between clusters.

In a multi-cluster environment, services need to be aware of each other's existence and location. Service discovery becomes more challenging when services are distributed across clusters, each with its own set of networking policies and configurations. Solutions like service meshes come into play here, offering tools to bridge these gaps, allowing services in different clusters to communicate as if they were in the same local network.

Impact of No Communication Between Clusters

Without effective communication between clusters, FusionCorp would face significant challenges. Each cluster would exist as an isolated island, unable to leverage the capabilities or data of services in other clusters. This isolation can lead to redundancy, where the same service is replicated in multiple clusters, leading to inefficient resource utilization and increased maintenance overhead.

The absence of inter-cluster communication also impacts the scalability and flexibility of the system. FusionCorp wouldn't be able to distribute workloads effectively across clusters, leading to potential bottlenecks and performance issues. For instance, if a cluster that handles data analytics is separate and unable to communicate with other clusters, the insights derived from its data cannot be effectively utilized by other services, undermining the potential benefits of a distributed architecture.

Moreover, disaster recovery and high availability strategies would be compromised. In a scenario where one cluster goes down, the services and data within that cluster would be inaccessible, with no immediate way for other clusters to take over its responsibilities. This scenario could lead to significant service disruptions and impact FusionCorp's business continuity.

As we progress in this chapter, we will explore how FusionCorp can implement and manage multi-cluster communication, focusing on practical approaches and solutions.

Setting up Linkerd for Multi-Cluster

Assuming that Linkerd is already installed in both Cluster-Alpha and Cluster-Beta, we will now configure these clusters for multi-cluster communication. This involves establishing trust and connectivity between the clusters.

Configure Cluster Gateways

Establishing Cross-Cluster Gateways

In a multi-cluster environment, a gateway is needed in each cluster to enable cross-cluster communication. These gateways will manage traffic between clusters, acting as the entry and exit points for cross-cluster communication.

Modify Linkerd Installation

Modify the Linkerd configuration to set up the gateways. This typically involves installing additional components and configuring service exports and imports.

For FusionCorp, apply the following changes to both Cluster-Alpha and Cluster-Beta:

```
linkerd --context=cluster-alpha multicluster install | kubectl --context=cluster-alpha apply -f -
linkerd --context=cluster-beta multicluster install | kubectl --context=cluster-beta apply -f -
```

This command sets up the necessary resources for multi-cluster communication in both clusters.

Link the Clusters

Generate and Apply Credentials

Generate a Linkerd multi-cluster link resource to connect Cluster-Beta to Cluster-Alpha:

```
linkerd --context=cluster-beta multicluster link --cluster-name beta-cluster |
kubectl --context=cluster-alpha apply -f -
```

This command creates the necessary credentials and configuration for Cluster-Alpha to connect to Cluster-Beta.

Service Mirroring

Mirror Services Across Clusters

Implement service mirroring to ensure that services running in one cluster can be discovered and accessed by services in another cluster. For instance, to mirror a service from Cluster-Beta to Cluster-Alpha:

```
kubectl --context=cluster-alpha apply -f beta-service-mirror.yaml
```

The beta-service-mirror.yaml file contains the definition for the service in Cluster-Beta to be mirrored in Cluster-Alpha.

This configuration enhances the capabilities and adaptability of FusionCorp's distributed microservices architecture by enabling services in different clusters to communicate without any hitches. To ensure stable and secure cross-cluster communication, the configuration should be monitored and validated on a regular basis.

Strategies for Multi-Cluster Communication

After successfully establishing a multi-cluster environment at FusionCorp with Linkerd, it is critical to comprehend and implement various strategies for effective multi-cluster communication. These strategies are critical for maximizing the benefits of a distributed architecture while also ensuring efficient, secure, and dependable inter-cluster communications.

Strategy 1: Traffic Management and Load Balancing

This strategy involves intelligently routing traffic between clusters based on factors like load, latency, and geographic location. By balancing the load evenly across clusters, FusionCorp can prevent any single cluster from being overwhelmed, thereby improving the overall system performance and availability. It also allows for better utilization of resources and can help in reducing latency for end-users by routing requests to the geographically nearest cluster.

Strategy 2: Service Failover and High Availability

Service failover involves configuring services in such a way that if a service or an entire cluster fails, the traffic is automatically redirected to a healthy instance of the service in another cluster. For FusionCorp, this strategy is essential for maintaining high availability. In the event of a cluster outage or service failure, the system can continue functioning seamlessly, ensuring uninterrupted service for users and minimizing downtime.

Strategy 3: Data Synchronization and Consistency

This strategy focuses on keeping data synchronized and consistent across clusters. It involves implementing mechanisms for data replication and consistency checks. Data synchronization ensures that all clusters have access to the latest data, which is critical for FusionCorp, especially if they operate in a read/write mode across clusters. It helps in maintaining data integrity and accuracy across the system.

Strategy 4: Cross-Cluster Security and Policy Enforcement

Security is paramount in multi-cluster communication. This strategy involves implementing consistent security policies, mutual TLS for encrypted communication, and access controls across clusters. For FusionCorp, ensuring that communication between clusters is secure and compliant with organizational policies is crucial. It prevents unauthorized access and data breaches, maintaining the confidentiality and integrity of the data being transmitted.

Strategy 5: Observability and Monitoring Across Clusters

Observability in a multi-cluster environment involves collecting and analyzing metrics, logs, and traces from all clusters to monitor the health and performance of services. Comprehensive observability allows FusionCorp to quickly identify and address issues across clusters, maintain optimal service performance, and make informed decisions based on real-time data.

Strategy 6: Deployment and Rollout Management

This strategy involves managing deployments across clusters, including canary releases and blue/green deployments, to ensure smooth rollouts of new features or updates. Controlled and phased rollouts across clusters minimize the risk of introducing bugs or issues into production. FusionCorp can test new releases under real-world conditions in one cluster before rolling them out system-wide, enhancing the stability and reliability of their services.

FusionCorp can fully benefit from their distributed Kubernetes environment by implementing these multi-cluster communication strategies. Each strategy is critical to improving the system's performance, reliability, security, and overall operational efficiency. Implementing them ensures that FusionCorp's services are robust, responsive, and resilient, regardless of the size or complexity of their operations.

Implementing Canary Rollouts Across Clusters

An effective strategy for controlled update deployment that minimizes the risk of releasing a new version to all users at once is to implement a canary rollout across clusters. The following is a practical example of using Linkerd to implement a canary rollout across Cluster-Alpha and Cluster-Beta, which are both used by FusionCorp.

Understanding Canary Rollouts

In a canary rollout, a new version of a service (the "canary") is gradually introduced to a small subset of users. The behavior of this version is closely monitored and compared against the current version. If the canary proves stable and performs well, it is gradually rolled out to more users, eventually replacing the old version.

Implementing Canary Rollout Across Clusters

Preparing the New Service Version

Assume FusionCorp has developed v2 of a payment-service, which they want to deploy across Cluster-Alpha and Cluster-Beta.

Deploy payment-service-v2 alongside the existing payment-service-v1 in both clusters. Ensure that both versions are configured to handle traffic and are integrated into the Linkerd mesh.

Set Up Traffic Split

Linkerd's TrafficSplit resource will be used to manage the traffic distribution between the two service versions.

Create a TrafficSplit definition to control the percentage of traffic that goes to each version.

```
apiVersion: split.smi-spec.io/v1alpha2
kind: TrafficSplit
metadata:
  name: payment-service-rollout
  namespace: default
```

```
spec:
  service: payment-service
  backends:
    - service: payment-service-v1
      weight: 90m
    - service: payment-service-v2
      weight: 10m
```

Initially, 10% of the traffic is directed to the new version (v2), and 90% to the existing version (v1).

Use kubectl to apply this configuration in both Cluster-Alpha and Cluster-Beta.

```
kubectl --context=cluster-alpha apply -f traffic-split-payment-service.yaml
kubectl --context=cluster-beta apply -f traffic-split-payment-service.yaml
```

Monitor the Canary

It's important to closely observe the new version's performance and compare it against the current version. Utilize Linkerd's dashboard to monitor the metrics for payment-service-v2 in both clusters. Pay attention to error rates, response times, and overall traffic volumes.

Collect feedback from the subset of users who are directed to the new version. This might include user-reported issues, log analysis, or automated error reporting.

Incrementally Increase Traffic to the Canary

If the new version performs well, gradually increase the traffic to it.

Adjust the weights in the TrafficSplit definition to increase the traffic to v2 incrementally. For example, an adjustment can be to increase v2 weight to 30m and decrease v1 weight to 70m. Apply these changes to both clusters.

Continuously monitor the performance as the traffic weight shifts. Ensure that v2 remains stable and performs as expected.

Full Rollout or Rollback

Based on the performance and stability of the new version, decide on a full rollout or a rollback.

If v2 is stable, continue to increase its weight in the TrafficSplit until all traffic is directed to it. Eventually, decommission v1.

If v2 introduces critical issues, roll back by adjusting the TrafficSplit to direct all traffic back to v1.

Finalize the Rollout
Once v2 is handling all traffic without issues, the rollout is complete. Remove the old version (v1) from the clusters. Update the TrafficSplit to reflect only the new version, or remove it if no longer necessary.

This entire approach not only safeguards the user experience but also provides valuable insights into the behavior of new deployments under real-world conditions.

Manage Stateful Apps in Multi-Cluster
Understanding Stateful Applications
Stateful apps save client data from one session to the next, resulting in a persistent state across time. This differs from stateless programs, which do not save user data across sessions. Managing stateful applications, particularly in a multi-cluster environment, is more difficult because you must ensure that the state is consistent throughout sessions, even when traffic is routed to various instances of the service in separate clusters.

Stateful applications typically involve databases or file systems where data is stored persistently. Examples include e-commerce sites that track user carts, or applications that require user login and maintain session information. In a multi-cluster setup, challenges include synchronizing data across clusters, handling database transactions, managing session state, and ensuring data integrity and consistency.

Managing Stateful Applications in Multi-Cluster
Strategy #1 - Data Replication
Ensure that data is replicated across clusters to maintain consistency. This can be done using tools like database replication mechanisms or distributed file systems.

For Example, if FusionCorp uses a SQL database in their stateful application, set up master-slave replication between clusters. Deploy primary database instances in one cluster (Cluster-Alpha) and replicas in another (Cluster-Beta). Use database-specific tools or Kubernetes operators for databases like PostgreSQL or MySQL to manage replication.

Strategy #2 - Stateful Sets and Persistent Volumes

Use StatefulSets for deploying stateful applications in Kubernetes. They provide stable, unique network identifiers and persistent storage for each instance. Use PVs and PVCs to manage storage for stateful applications. Consider dynamic provisioning of storage using StorageClass to automate PV creation as per the requirements of the StatefulSet.

Strategy #3 - Session Affinity

Configure session affinity in your load balancers to ensure that requests from the same client are directed to the same service instance. In Linkerd, session affinity can be achieved through service profiles or by configuring load balancing at the ingress controller.

Strategy #4 - Centralized State Management

For some use cases, it may be beneficial to centralize state management in a single cluster or an external service. Use services like Redis or Memcached for session state, centralized configuration management systems, or cloud-based databases.

Strategy #5 - Cross-Cluster Communication

Ensure that the application logic is designed to handle cross-cluster communication for state synchronization. Use Linkerd for secure and reliable cross-cluster communication to access databases or other stateful services across clusters.

Strategy #6 - Backup and Disaster Recovery

Implement a robust backup strategy for stateful data. Regularly back up databases and stateful data to a centralized, secure storage location. Develop and regularly test a disaster recovery plan to handle data loss or corruption scenarios.

Any technology business, including FusionCorp, must assure data consistency and availability across clusters to protect the integrity of stateful applications. Regular backups and a good disaster recovery plan are critical for protecting against data loss. FusionCorp can easily manage their stateful applications across different clusters by leveraging Kubernetes' StatefulSets, PVs, and PVCs, as well as integrating with secure communication solutions such as Linkerd.

Traffic Mirroring for Testing in Production

Understanding Traffic Mirroring in Production

Traffic mirroring, also known as shadowing, is a technique for testing and evaluating changes in a production environment without affecting actual users. The process entails redirecting real-time traffic from a live service in production to a replica of that service. This mirrored service is usually a new version or configuration of the application under test.

It's particularly useful for performance testing, bug hunting, and capacity planning. Since the mirrored traffic is actual user data, it provides accurate insights into how the new version behaves under realistic conditions. Developers also receive immediate feedback on their changes, allowing for rapid iteration and improvement.

Benefits

- The primary benefit is that it enables testing in production without any risk to the user experience. Users continue to interact with the stable version of the application.
- Mirroring real traffic gives a clear picture of how the system performs under actual load conditions, which is often hard to simulate in test environments.
- It helps in identifying issues that may not surface in a staged environment, like race conditions, memory leaks, or database bottlenecks.

Implementing Traffic Mirroring in Production

Deploy the Test Version

Deploy the test version of the checkout-service, say checkout-service-test, in the same cluster as the production service. Ensure that this version is similar to the production version but configured for testing (e.g., connected to a test database).

Modify the Service Configuration

Using Linkerd, configure traffic mirroring in the service profile of checkout-service. Update the service profile to mirror a portion of the traffic to checkout-service-test.

```
apiVersion: linkerd.io/v1alpha2
kind: ServiceProfile
metadata:
  name: checkout-service.default.svc.cluster.local
  namespace: default
spec:
  routes:
    - name: mirror-checkout-test
      condition:
        method: GET
        pathRegex: /checkout
```

```
mirror:
   serviceName: checkout-service-test.default.svc.cluster.local
   percentage: 0.5
```

This configuration mirrors 50% of the GET requests to /checkout to the checkout-service-test.

Deploy the Service Profile
Apply the updated service profile in Cluster-Alpha:

```
kubectl apply -f checkout-service-profile.yaml
```

Observe the Test Service
Monitor checkout-service-test using Linkerd's dashboard to analyze how it handles the mirrored traffic. Look for any discrepancies in performance, errors, or other issues when compared to the production service.

Based on observations, make necessary adjustments to the checkout-service-test. Continue mirroring traffic until satisfied with the service's performance and stability.

Remove Mirroring
Once testing is complete, remove the traffic mirroring configuration from the service profile. Optionally, decommission the checkout-service-test if it's no longer needed.

By implementing traffic mirroring, FusionCorp can validate updates under real traffic conditions without impacting their users. This approach enables them to gain valuable insights into the performance and stability of new features or configurations, leading to more reliable and robust services.

Multi-Cluster Monitoring and Observability
Understanding Observability in Linkerd

Observability in Linkerd is built around the concept of providing comprehensive insight into the service mesh's operations without the need for additional instrumentation or configuration. It's designed to be automatic and low-overhead, making it an ideal solution for dynamic and complex environments like FusionCorp's.

Following are the key features of Observability:
- Automatic Metrics Collection: Linkerd automatically collects a wide range of metrics from

the data plane (service proxies) without any manual intervention.
- Real-Time Traffic Monitoring: It provides real-time visibility into the traffic flow within the mesh, including request volumes, success rates, and latencies.
- Distributed Tracing: While not a core feature, Linkerd can integrate with external systems like Jaeger or Zipkin to provide distributed tracing capabilities.
- Service-Level and Route-Level Metrics: Metrics are available at both the service and route levels, allowing for detailed analysis.
- Dashboard and Grafana Integration: Linkerd comes with a web dashboard for visualizing service metrics and integrates with Grafana for advanced data visualization and analysis.
- Alerting and Anomaly Detection: While Linkerd itself doesn't provide alerting, its integration with Prometheus allows users to set up alerts based on the metrics collected.

Traffic and Performance Metrics

- Request Volume: Monitor the total number of requests per second to each service. Helps in understanding the load and identifying peak usage times.
- Success Rate: Observing the percentage of successful requests vs. failures. Critical for identifying services that are experiencing issues or are unreliable.
- Request Duration: Monitoring the latency of requests, which is essential for maintaining a responsive user experience. Helps in pinpointing services that are slow or becoming performance bottlenecks.
- Top-Line Service Metrics: Observing overall service health metrics such as request rates, error rates, and latencies.

Resource Utilization

- CPU and Memory Usage: Tracking the resource consumption of each proxy instance helps in identifying services that may be resource-intensive or leaking resources.
- Proxy Performance: Monitoring the performance of Linkerd proxies themselves, ensuring they are operating efficiently and not adding undue latency.

Network and Traffic Patterns

- Traffic Patterns: Understanding how traffic flows through the mesh, which services communicate most, and the nature of these interactions.
- Ingress/Egress Traffic: Observing traffic entering and leaving the mesh, useful for understanding external dependencies and user entry points.

Reliability Metrics

- Error Rates: Monitoring the rate of different types of errors (4xx, 5xx HTTP responses) to identify potential issues at the service level.
- Service Dependencies and Failures: Observing dependencies between services and how

failures in one service affect others.

- Retries and Failovers: Tracking the retry attempts and failovers, which can indicate underlying problems with service stability or network issues.

Tracing and Diagnostic Data

- Distributed Tracing Data: (If integrated with Jaeger/Zipkin) Analyzing trace data to understand the request flow and latency contributions from various services.
- Logs and Events: While Linkerd doesn't directly handle logging, integrating with a logging system allows for correlating logs with observed metrics.

Linkerd's observability offers FusionCorp with a full set of tools and metrics for monitoring and intimately understanding the state of their services. Observability not only helps with troubleshooting and problem resolution rapidly, but it also plays an important part in proactive performance management and system optimization.

Linkerd Performance Indicators

Setting up and using important indicators or metrics in Linkerd entails exploiting Linkerd's automated metrics collecting and combining it with monitoring tools such as Prometheus and Grafana. With this configuration, FusionCorp will be able to effectively monitor the performance and health of their services.

Following is a practical way to establishing these metrics:

Integrate with Prometheus

Linkerd comes with its own instance of Prometheus, which automatically collects and stores metrics from the service mesh.

Access Prometheus

Access the Prometheus instance installed with Linkerd. It is typically deployed in the linkerd namespace. You can access the Prometheus dashboard using:

```
linkerd -n linkerd dashboard &
```

Navigate to the Prometheus dashboard through the Linkerd web interface.

Configure Prometheus Scraping:

If FusionCorp uses their own Prometheus instance, configure it to scrape metrics from Linkerd. The scrape configuration might look something like this:

```
scrape_configs:
- job_name: 'linkerd'
  kubernetes_sd_configs:
  - role: pod
  relabel_configs:
  - source_labels:
      - __meta_kubernetes_pod_container_port_name
    action: keep
    regex: ^linkerd-proxy$
```

This configuration ensures Prometheus collects metrics exposed by the Linkerd proxies.

Setup Grafana Dashboards

Access Grafana
Linkerd provides pre-configured Grafana dashboards for visualizing the metrics it collects. Access Grafana through the Linkerd dashboard, which has dashboards pre-configured to display Linkerd metrics.

Custom Dashboards
If FusionCorp has specific requirements, they can customize or create new dashboards in Grafana.One can import or create dashboards that reflect the KPIs and metrics crucial for their services.

Monitoring Key Metrics and Indicators

- Regularly check service-level metrics such as request volume, success rate, and request duration. Use Grafana dashboards for an aggregated view or drill down into specific services for detailed analysis.
- Monitor CPU and memory utilization of the Linkerd proxies to ensure they are not consuming excessive resources. Set up alerts in Grafana or Prometheus for unusual spikes in resource usage.
- Keep an eye on error rates and types of errors (4xx, 5xx responses) to identify potential issues in services. Set up alerts for high error rates which might indicate problems with specific services.
- Analyze traffic patterns to understand the flow of requests through the system. Look for changes in patterns that might indicate issues or potential bottlenecks.

Setup Alerts in Prometheus

- Set up alert rules in Prometheus for key metrics. For example, create an alert for high error rates or latency spikes. Prometheus alerts can be integrated with FusionCorp's incident management system to notify on-call engineers.
- Conduct regular reviews of the collected metrics to understand the health and performance of the services over time. Use insights from these reviews for capacity planning, performance optimization, and identifying areas for improvement.
- By configuring these metrics and indications in Linkerd, one can obtain thorough insight into the efficiency, well-being, and dependability of their microservices. With the help of Grafana's actionable insights and Prometheus's alerts, they are able to keep their service infrastructure running smoothly, reliably, and quickly.

Best Practices - Multi-Cluster Management

Managing multi-cluster environments, as illustrated in FusionCorp's case, demands a set of best practices to ensure efficiency, security, and reliability. Following is a comprehensive look at these practices, going beyond mere listing to provide a deeper understanding of each.

#1 - Comprehensive Monitoring and Observability

In a multi-cluster setup, tracking the performance, health, and metrics of services across all clusters is crucial. It helps in identifying issues, optimizing resource usage, and understanding traffic patterns. Utilize tools like Linkerd's dashboard, Prometheus, and Grafana for monitoring. Ensure metrics are collected uniformly across all clusters and set up centralized dashboards for a holistic view.

#2 - Consistent Security and Access Management

Consistency in security policies and access controls across clusters is essential to prevent breaches and unauthorized access. Implement uniform security policies, mutual TLS, and role-based access controls. Use service meshes like Linkerd to manage security policies and ensure they are consistently applied across clusters.

#3 - Efficient Traffic Management

Properly managing traffic between clusters is vital to optimize performance and ensure high availability. It involves intelligent routing, load balancing, and failover strategies. Use Linkerd's TrafficSplit for controlled rollouts and canary deployments. Set up load balancing and failover mechanisms to distribute traffic effectively and maintain service availability.

#4 - Disaster Recovery and High Availability

Preparing for failures and ensuring high availability are critical in a multi-cluster environment to prevent service disruptions. Implement a robust disaster recovery plan, including data backup and restoration strategies. Use replication and failover techniques to maintain service availability across clusters.

#5 - Data Synchronization and Consistency

Ensuring data consistency across clusters, especially for stateful applications, is vital to maintain integrity and provide a seamless user experience. Implement data replication methods suitable for your databases and storage systems. Regularly check for data integrity and consistency issues.

#6 - Streamlined Deployment Processes

A streamlined and consistent deployment process across clusters reduces errors and simplifies management. Standardize deployment pipelines using CI/CD tools like Jenkins. Ensure configurations and deployment scripts are uniform across clusters to minimize discrepancies.

#7 - Regular Policy and Configuration Audits

Regular audits help in maintaining the consistency of configurations and policies across clusters and identifying discrepancies. Periodically review and audit network policies, security configurations, and resource allocations. Use automated tools where possible to ensure consistency.

#8 - Embracing Automation and Orchestration

Automation reduces manual errors and streamlines operations, essential in complex multi-cluster environments. Automate routine tasks like deployments, scaling, and backups. Use Kubernetes operators and other orchestration tools to manage cluster operations.

Adopting these best practices allows FusionCorp to effectively manage their multi-cluster environment. It ensures operational efficiency, enhances security, maintains high service availability, and provides a consistent and reliable user experience. Each best practice plays a pivotal role in addressing the unique challenges of managing multiple Kubernetes clusters.

Summary

Chapter 6, "Multi-Cluster Communication and Rollouts," examined the complex dynamics of managing and orchestrating services across many Kubernetes clusters, a common scenario in complex companies like FusionCorp. The chapter began with an in-depth learning of the importance of multi-cluster communication, highlighting how different clusters must connect fluidly in order to efficiently use distributed resources, assure service continuity, and improve disaster recovery capabilities. It emphasized the difficulties and consequences of not having efficient communication paths between clusters, such as isolated data silos, poor resource utilization, and reduced fault tolerance, which could greatly impede operational efficiency and scalability.

The chapter then moved on to the practical aspects of implementing Linkerd for multi-cluster environments, demonstrating how FusionCorp may facilitate cross-cluster connectivity by enabling gateways and service mirroring. This configuration allows services in different clusters to discover and communicate with one another as if they were in the same cluster, improving the overall functionality and dependability of the distributed system. We then looked at different solutions for effective multi-cluster communication, including intelligent traffic management, load balancing, data synchronization, and uniform policy enforcement across clusters. These approaches are critical for ensuring system performance, data integrity, and security in a complex multi-cluster environment.

The chapter's conclusion included practical instructions on creating canary rollouts and managing stateful applications across many clusters. Canary rollouts, which involve incremental traffic shifting to new service versions, allow FusionCorp to implement changes with little risk by exploiting real-world user traffic to assess the impact of new releases. To ensure data consistency and service reliability, stateful applications must be managed carefully, which includes data replication, persistent storage, and session management. The chapter concludes by learning traffic mirroring for testing in production environments, a technique that enables FusionCorp to test new features under real-world conditions without harming user experience. FusionCorp uses these insights to traverse the intricacies of multi-cluster systems, ensuring that their services are robust, durable, and responsive to changing business and technological landscapes.

CHAPTER 7: PROGRESSIVE DELIVERY AND INGRESS INTEGRATION

Introduction to Progressive Delivery

Overview

This chapter focuses on an advanced deployment approach that has become an essential component of contemporary DevOps practices, particularly in cloud-native environments such as FusionCorp. Continuous delivery approaches have evolved into progressive delivery, which provides greater granular control over the release process when compared to continuous delivery. A method known as progressive delivery is one that involves the gradual deployment of updates, as opposed to the simultaneous release of all updates to all users. It extends the principles of continuous delivery by providing fine-grained control over the deployment process. This makes it possible for features to be rolled out to a small group of users first, and then gradually to larger segments of the user base. When using this strategy, the risk that is involved with delivering new software versions is reduced, and a safety net is provided for promptly fixing any problems that may arise.

Core Components of Progressive Delivery

When we talk about the fundamental components of progressive delivery, it's like having a toolbox that ensures software upgrades run smoothly and safely. Let us split them down into understandable chunks.

Canary Releases

Imagine delivering a new feature, but instead of launching it to everyone at once, you begin small. You initially make it available to a small number of users. This is similar to testing the waters. If this small group has no problems with the new function and appreciates it, you can progressively roll it out to additional users. This strategy helps detect problems early on, reducing the impact on all users.

Feature Flags

This is a useful technique that allows you to turn specific features on or off without having to publish new code to your servers. Consider it a remote control for your app's functionalities. You can easily control which features are available to users. This gives you a lot of freedom and can be quite useful for testing new features or making adjustments in real time.

A/B Testing

This involves comparing two versions of your program to find which one performs better. You may have one version of a page or feature that appears or functions slightly differently than another. One part of your users will see version A, while another will see version B. You then determine which version more successfully engages users or achieves your business objectives. It's like running a scientific experiment to determine the greatest customer experience.

Blue/Green Deployments

This strategy focuses on reducing downtime and risk when delivering new versions of your program. You have two identical production environments: Blue and Green. At any one time, only one of these settings is operational, handling all traffic. When you're ready to release a new version, you push it to the inactive environment. Once you're certain that the new version is stable, you redirect traffic from the current live environment to the new one. If something goes wrong, you may immediately go back to the previous version, guaranteeing that your users receive uninterrupted service.

Each of these above components is critical to the progressive delivery method, providing a safety net as you add new features and upgrades to your program.

Potential Benefits of Progressive Delivery

When exploring the possible benefits of progressive delivery, it becomes evident how this method can radically improve software release and management.

Reduced Deployment Risk

This feature of progressive delivery is similar to taking measured steps. By presenting changes in stages, the overall process becomes less intimidating. Consider crossing a brook with stepping stones rather than attempting to leap across in one go. This strategy considerably reduces the likelihood of experiencing catastrophic disruptions or system-wide failures. Each tiny release serves as a test in itself, ensuring that any possible flaws are limited and do not evolve into larger difficulties.

Enhanced User Experience

Progressive delivery is similar to having a constant dialogue with your users. You can get rapid feedback by releasing features to a specific section of people. This is crucial since it allows you to see how real people interact with the new features, what they enjoy, and what may be improved. Because of this direct connection to user emotions, any negative consequences are promptly identified and corrected, resulting in a better refined user experience.

Faster Recovery from Issues

If a problem arises, its impact is limited to a smaller audience, and the path to recovery is clearer and faster. It's like having a safety net. Because just a small percentage of the user population is affected, rolling back or resolving the issue becomes a more doable operation, avoiding widespread user displeasure and potential reputational damage.

Improved Release Confidence

Gradual releases provide a certain peace of mind. It's like gradually cranking up the light; you have time to adjust to the change. This controlled method ensures that you can be confident on the system's stability at any point during the release process. It enables teams to validate each phase before going on to the next, resulting in a stable and dependable deployment.

Efficient Resource Utilization

Being resource-conscious is another aspect of progressive delivery. Monitoring how new features are received and used allows you to better plan and manage resources. This entails scaling up or down according to actual user demand and engagement, resulting in more effective operations and cost savings.

Contribution to DevOps and Cloud Professionals

- Facilitating Continuous Integration/Continuous Deployment (CI/CD): Progressive delivery is a natural extension of CI/CD practices, providing more control and safety. It allows DevOps teams to integrate new features and updates continuously without disrupting the service.

- Enabling Faster Iteration: DevOps teams can quickly iterate on software features, test them in production-like environments, and gather feedback. This rapid iteration cycle is crucial in today's fast-paced development environments.

- Enhancing Observability and Monitoring: Progressive delivery requires robust monitoring and logging to track the impact of new releases. This leads to improved observability practices, helping teams to better understand their systems.

- Simplifying Compliance and Security: By releasing changes gradually, it's easier to ensure compliance with various regulations. Security checks can be more thorough and contextual for each release phase.

- Promoting Experimentation: Progressive delivery encourages experimenting with new features and ideas, knowing that any negative impact can be contained and managed.

- Better Resource Management in the Cloud: Cloud professionals can leverage progressive delivery to optimize resource utilization in the cloud, scaling up or down based on the phase of the rollout.

Progressive delivery represents a significant evolution in how software is delivered and managed. It empowers FusionCorp's DevOps and cloud teams to deploy updates in a controlled, measured way, significantly reducing deployment risks and enhancing the overall quality of the service. As we move forward in this chapter, we will explore the practical implementation of progressive delivery strategies and how to integrate them effectively with ingress controllers in a Kubernetes environment, further amplifying the benefits of this approach in FusionCorp's operations.

Pair Linkerd with Kubernetes Ingress

The combination of Linkerd and Kubernetes ingress is an advantageous approach and a powerful combination that enables you to exploit the characteristics of Linkerd, such as traffic splitting and observability, in conjunction with the ingress controllers of Kubernetes for the purpose of effective traffic management.

Ingress in Kubernetes with Linkerd

Ingress in Kubernetes is a resource that manages external access to services within a cluster, typically HTTP/HTTPS traffic. It provides load balancing, SSL termination, and name-based virtual hosting.

Linkerd, when paired with an ingress controller, enhances the ingress with service mesh features like secure communication, observability, and fine-grained traffic control.

Steps to Pair Linkerd with Kubernetes Ingress

Choose and Install an Ingress Controller
Choose an ingress controller that best fits FusionCorp's needs. Popular options include NGINX Ingress Controller, Traefik, and HAProxy.

For the below sample program, we should use NGINX Ingress Controller.

Install the NGINX Ingress Controller in your cluster. If using Helm, the command might look like:

```
helm install nginx-ingress stable/nginx-ingress
```

Integrate Linkerd with the Ingress Controller
To integrate the ingress controller with Linkerd, inject Linkerd's data plane proxies into the ingress controller's pods. For NGINX, you would annotate the deployment:

```
kubectl annotate deployment nginx-ingress-controller linkerd.io/inject=enabled
```

This step ensures that the ingress traffic goes through Linkerd's proxies, enabling you to leverage Linkerd's features for ingress traffic.

Configure Ingress Resources
Create Ingress resources to define how external traffic should be routed to your services. An

example Ingress resource might look like:

```
apiVersion: networking.k8s.io/v1
kind: Ingress
metadata:
  name: example-ingress
  namespace: default
spec:
  rules:
  - host: www.example.com
    http:
      paths:
      - path: /
        pathType: Prefix
        backend:
          service:
            name: example-service
            port:
              number: 80
```

Monitor and Optimize Traffic

Once the ingress is integrated with Linkerd, use the Linkerd dashboard to observe and monitor the ingress traffic. This includes metrics like request volume, success rates, and latencies.

Based on the metrics observed, you might need to fine-tune your ingress configurations, such as adjusting load balancing rules or optimizing TLS settings.

Implement Advanced Traffic Control

Implement advanced traffic control strategies like canary releases using Linkerd's TrafficSplit resource. This allows you to gradually shift traffic from one service version to another. You may use the ingress controller to direct a subset of traffic to different service versions based on criteria like HTTP headers or cookies, facilitating A/B testing.

Ensure Security

Configure SSL/TLS termination at the ingress level for secure HTTPS traffic. Ensure that communication between the ingress controller and backend services is also secured using Linkerd's automatic mTLS.

By injecting Linkerd into the ingress controller, FusionCorp gains access to Linkerd's observability, security, and traffic control functionalities for incoming traffic. This configuration enables them to properly monitor incoming traffic, deploy canaries, and assure secure connection.

Manage Traffic Split for Progressive Delivery

A fundamental principle of progressive delivery, traffic splitting is essential for coordinating the distribution of traffic across various service versions in a Kubernetes environment. It is especially relevant for enterprises such as FusionCorp that want to use advanced deployment tactics. Traffic splitting is the ability to divide network traffic between various service versions. This method is used to test new features, make canary releases, and set up blue/green deployments.

Purpose of Traffic Split

Traffic splitting allows FusionCorp to gradually introduce a new version of a service to a subset of their user base, thereby minimizing the risk associated with deploying new software versions. It enables testing new features under real-world conditions, providing valuable feedback on performance and user experience without fully committing the change to all users. In case of any issues, traffic can be quickly rerouted back to the stable version, ensuring service continuity and minimal impact on the end users.

Implementing Traffic Split with Linkerd

Linkerd's traffic split capability is ideal for implementing progressive delivery strategies. It allows FusionCorp to distribute traffic between different service versions based on predefined rules. Assume FusionCorp wants to introduce a new version (v2) of their inventory-service and use traffic splitting to gradually shift traffic from v1 to v2.

Deploy New Service Version

Deploy the new version (v2) alongside the existing version (v1) in the same Kubernetes namespace. Ensure both versions are configured to handle traffic and are integrated into the Linkerd service mesh.

Define and Apply a TrafficSplit Resource

Define a TrafficSplit resource to manage the distribution of traffic between v1 and v2.

```yaml
apiVersion: split.smi-spec.io/v1alpha2
kind: TrafficSplit
metadata:
  name: inventory-service-split
  namespace: default
spec:
  service: inventory-service
  backends:
    - service: inventory-service-v1
      weight: 500m
    - service: inventory-service-v2
      weight: 500m
```

This configuration starts with distributing traffic evenly (50-50) between v1 and v2.

Then, you use kubectl to apply the TrafficSplit configuration:

```
kubectl apply -f traffic-split-inventory-service.yaml
```

Monitor the Traffic Distribution

Monitor the traffic distribution and performance metrics for both v1 and v2 using the Linkerd dashboard. Observe metrics such as response times, error rates, and success rates.

Incrementally Adjust Traffic Weight

Based on the performance and stability of v2, gradually modify the TrafficSplit weights to shift more traffic to the new version. For example, update the TrafficSplit to direct 70% of traffic to v2 and 30% to v1.

Keep a close eye on the metrics and user feedback. If v2 performs well, continue increasing its traffic share. If issues arise with v2, quickly adjust the TrafficSplit to redirect traffic back to v1.

Complete the Rollout

Once confident in the stability and performance of v2, shift 100% of the traffic to the new version. Eventually, decommission v1 of inventory-service.

This method considerably reduces the risks involved with delivering new software versions in a dynamic, user-centric business environment. They may use Linkerd's traffic split capabilities to test new features in production, get real-time feedback, and guarantee that every new deployment meets their high quality and performance criteria before full adoption.

Introduction to Flagger

Overview

Flagger is a progressive delivery tool designed to automate the release process in Kubernetes environments. It works by automating the promotion of canary deployments using metrics from observability tools. Flagger can be integrated with service meshes like Linkerd, Istio, and others, making it a versatile choice for managing complex deployments.

Role in Progressive Delivery

Flagger extends Kubernetes capabilities for advanced deployment strategies like canary releases, A/B testing, and blue/green deployments. It evaluates the health of your application based on metrics before progressing to the next step, effectively reducing the risk of introducing new software versions.

Integration with Service Meshes

Flagger leverages service mesh capabilities to control the traffic flow during deployment processes. It uses the mesh's features for traffic shifting and real-time monitoring.

Installing Flagger

To install Flagger in FusionCorp's environment, where Linkerd is already deployed, follow these steps:

- Ensure you have a Kubernetes cluster with Linkerd installed.
- Install Helm, a package manager for Kubernetes, to simplify the installation of Flagger.
- Add Flagger's Helm Repository:

```
helm repo add flagger https://flagger.app
```

- Install Flagger in the linkerd namespace where Linkerd is deployed.

```
helm upgrade -i flagger flagger/flagger \
  --namespace=linkerd \
  --set crd.create=true \
```

```
--set meshProvider=linkerd \
--set metricsServer=http://linkerd-prometheus:9090
```

This command installs Flagger and configures it to use Linkerd as the mesh provider and Linkerd's Prometheus for metrics.

Flagger for Blue and Green Deployments

Blue/Green deployment is a strategy where two versions of an application are run simultaneously, with only one serving live production traffic at a time. The new version (green) is deployed alongside the old version (blue) but does not receive any user traffic. Once the green version is fully tested and deemed stable, traffic is switched from the blue to the green version.

Flagger automates the process of gradually shifting traffic from the blue to the green environment based on predefined metrics and criteria. It integrates with Kubernetes and service meshes to manage this process effectively.

Implementation of Blue/Green Deployment with Flagger

Ensure you have a Kubernetes deployment and a corresponding service. For instance, a frontend deployment and a frontend-svc service.

Preparing the Deployment and Service

The deployment manifest for the frontend application should be defined. This manifest includes the specifications for the application pods. A corresponding Kubernetes service (frontend-svc) directs traffic to the pods managed by the frontend deployment.

Setting Up Flagger

The Canary custom resource (CR) defines the blue/green deployment process. The CR includes details such as the target deployment, metrics for evaluation, and service names for routing traffic.

```
apiVersion: flagger.app/v1beta1
kind: Canary
metadata:
  name: frontend
  namespace: default
spec:
```

```
provider: linkerd
targetRef:
  apiVersion: apps/v1
  kind: Deployment
  name: frontend
service:
  port: 80
  targetPort: 8080
analysis:
  interval: 1m
  threshold: 5
  iterations: 10
  metrics:
  - name: request-success-rate
    thresholdRange:
      min: 99
    interval: 1m
  - name: request-duration
    thresholdRange:
      max: 500
    interval: 1m
  blueGreen:
    previewService: frontend-preview
    activeService: frontend-primary
```

This configuration tells Flagger to manage the frontend deployment using a blue/green strategy. The frontend-primary service routes traffic to the current version, while the frontend-preview service is used for the new version under testing.

Deploying New Version (Green Environment)

Make changes to the frontend deployment, such as updating the application version or configuration. Deploy the updated frontend application to the cluster. Flagger detects the deployment update and starts the blue/green process. Initially, all traffic is still routed to the blue environment (frontend-primary). Flagger routes internal (or a subset of) traffic to the green environment (frontend-preview) for testing based on the Canary CR. The green environment is monitored against the defined metrics. If the new version is stable and meets the criteria, Flagger prepares to switch traffic.

Traffic Switching

Upon successful evaluation, Flagger shifts production traffic from the blue to the green environment. The frontend-primary service now points to the new version of the application. If, at any point, the new version fails to meet the criteria, Flagger can automatically revert the traffic back to the blue environment, minimizing risk.

Finalizing the Deployment

Once the green environment is successfully serving production traffic and is stable, the rollout is complete. The previous version (blue environment) can be decommissioned or kept as a rollback option for a period. Flagger allows FusionCorp to implement advanced deployment strategies with minimal manual intervention, reducing the risks associated with deploying new versions.

Rollback Strategies in Progressive Delivery

Rollback solutions in progressive delivery are essential for assuring service stability and providing a high-quality user experience. These solutions provide a safety net, allowing for speedy recovery if new deployments encounter unexpected challenges or have a detrimental impact on users. These tactics are critical components of a strong deployment strategy, particularly in contexts where dependability and user experience are important.

Key Rollback Strategies

Automatic Rollback

This strategy uses real-time monitoring data to trigger a rollback. If key performance indicators (KPIs) fall below certain thresholds after a new deployment, the system automatically reverts to the previous version. For instance, if the error rate or latency spikes significantly post-deployment, an automated system can instantly roll back to the stable version.

Manual Rollback

Manual rollback is a controlled process where the operations team reverts the system to a previous state based on their judgment. This strategy is often used when automated metrics might not fully capture the issue, or in complex scenarios where a careful, step-by-step rollback is necessary. It requires a thorough understanding of the system and the changes introduced by the new deployment.

Canary Rollback

In a canary deployment, if the canary (the new version released to a small subset of users) shows any signs of failure or underperformance, it's rolled back, while the majority of the traffic continues to flow to the stable version. Canary rollbacks are often automated, relying on predefined criteria for performance and stability.

Blue/Green Rollback

In blue/green deployments, the 'green' environment with the new version runs in parallel with the 'blue' environment hosting the stable version. If issues arise in the green environment, traffic is immediately routed back to the blue environment. This strategy allows for near-instantaneous rollbacks with minimal user impact.

Implementation with Flagger and Linkerd

Given FusionCorp's setup with Linkerd and the potential integration with tools like Flagger, these rollback strategies can be effectively implemented. We shall delve into a practical example, focusing on implementing an automatic rollback strategy using Flagger and Linkerd. This example will help illustrate how FusionCorp can safeguard their deployment process.

Imagine FusionCorp has an application called product-service. They're about to roll out a new version (v2) and want to ensure that if anything goes wrong post-deployment, the system will automatically revert to the previous stable version (v1).

Define Canary Resource

Create a Canary custom resource for product-service. This resource outlines the criteria for a successful deployment and the conditions for an automatic rollback.

For example:

```
apiVersion: flagger.app/v1beta1
kind: Canary
metadata:
  name: product-service
  namespace: default
```

```yaml
spec:
  provider: linkerd
  targetRef:
    apiVersion: apps/v1
    kind: Deployment
    name: product-service
  service:
    port: 8080
  analysis:
    interval: 1m
    threshold: 3
    iterations: 5
    metrics:
    - name: request-success-rate
      thresholdRange:
        min: 99
      interval: 1m
    - name: request-duration
      thresholdRange:
        max: 500
      interval: 1m
```

This configuration monitors product-service post-update. If the success rate drops below 99% or request duration exceeds 500 ms, Flagger will initiate a rollback after 3 failed checks within 5 minutes.

Apply the Canary Configuration

Deploy this Canary resource in the Kubernetes cluster:

```
kubectl apply -f product-service-canary.yaml
```

Update product-service to v2

Update the deployment manifest for product-service to roll out the new version. Once deployed, Flagger starts monitoring product-service based on the defined Canary rules.

Observe the Rollout

Using Linkerd's dashboard, observe the rollout. Pay attention to request success rate and latency. Flagger also monitors these metrics based on the Canary definition.

If product-service v2 fails to meet the Canary criteria (e.g., the error rate is too high or latency is unacceptable), Flagger automatically triggers a rollback. Traffic is rerouted back to the stable v1 version, mitigating the risk of the new version affecting users.

Analyze the Failure

FusionCorp's team analyzes why v2 failed the Canary checks. This could involve diving into logs, metrics, or user feedback. Once the issues are identified and fixed, v2 of product-service can be redeployed and reevaluated.

This strategy ensures that new versions of their services are thoroughly evaluated under real traffic conditions, and any potential negative impact is swiftly mitigated. The use of Canary resources provides a clear, declarative approach to defining the criteria for successful deployments and the conditions under which an automatic rollback should be triggered, thereby maintaining service stability and a high-quality user experience.

Best Practices - Progressive Delivery

Navigating the world of progressive delivery takes more than just understanding the tools and technology; it also needs adopting a set of best practices that assure successful, risk-managed deployments.

Following are some critical principles that FusionCorp and other organizations should adopt to excel at progressive delivery.

#1 - Gradual Rollout of Features

Rather than deploying a new feature to all users at once, it's more prudent to roll it out gradually. Begin by exposing the feature to a small, controlled group of users, and then incrementally increase the exposure based on feedback and performance metrics. This approach minimizes the impact of potential issues and allows for gathering real user feedback before a full-scale rollout.

#2 - Insightful Tracking

Monitoring is the backbone of progressive delivery. It's essential to have a comprehensive observability framework in place that tracks a wide array of metrics, including user behavior, application performance, and system health.

Tools like Linkerd and Prometheus can be instrumental in providing real-time insights into how new releases are performing, allowing for quick adjustments or rollbacks if necessary.

#3 - Thorough Validation
Before even beginning a progressive rollout, thorough testing in a pre-production environment that closely mimics the real-world setup is crucial. This includes load testing, security testing, and user acceptance testing.

Ensuring that the new release is as bug-free as possible before it enters the progressive delivery pipeline reduces the likelihood of encountering major issues during rollout.

#4 - Safety Net
Implement automated rollback mechanisms, like those offered by Flagger, which can revert to the previous version of a service if certain conditions are met. These conditions might include an unacceptable increase in error rates or a significant drop in performance metrics. Automated rollbacks act as a safety net, ensuring that any negative impact on the system is quickly contained.

#5 - Dynamic Control
Feature flags offer a dynamic way to enable or disable features without redeploying the application. This can be particularly useful for testing new features in a live environment or quickly disabling them if they exhibit unexpected behavior. Feature flagging allows for more granular control over the release process and can be a valuable tool in the progressive delivery arsenal.

These best practices into progressive delivery strategy can significantly enhance the success rate of their deployments. This approach not only ensures a smoother rollout of new features but also aligns closely with the broader goals of risk management, user satisfaction, and operational excellence.

Summary

For cutting-edge cloud-native setups like FusionCorp, this chapter, "Progressive Delivery and Ingress Integration," offered an in-depth look at the sophisticated deployment approach. It began with an overview of progressive delivery, a method that builds on the ideas of continuous delivery but provides greater control and safety. Progressive delivery, as previously described, entails gradually distributing changes using techniques such as canary releases, feature flags, and A/B testing. This method lowers the risk of new software versions by a large amount. It also lets FusionCorp try new features in real life and get feedback right away. The primary advantage is the ability to reduce user impact while continuing to innovate and develop.

The chapter went into greater detail on Linkerd's interface with Kubernetes' ingress, which is critical for managing external access to services within FusionCorp's clusters. FusionCorp may use the observability, security, and traffic control aspects of the service mesh for inbound external traffic by combining Linkerd and Kubernetes ingress controllers. We learned how to put this configuration into practice, emphasizing the significance of monitoring and optimizing network flow. Furthermore, the notion of traffic splitting was learned, emphasizing its importance in progressive delivery for safely controlling the release of new versions. We demonstrated through real situations how FusionCorp can use Linkerd's traffic split capabilities to do controlled rollouts, guaranteeing that each new deployment meets their rigorous quality criteria. The chapter also introduced Flagger, a tool for automating the release process in Kubernetes environments, and learned how it may be used to accomplish blue/green deployments. FusionCorp can use Flagger to smoothly manage the transition between new and existing versions of their services, optimizing their deployment strategy.

This chapter gave significant insights into best practices for managing progressive delivery, emphasizing the necessity of gradual feature rollouts, complete monitoring, rigorous testing in pre-production settings, and automated rollback methods. These practices are not simply ideas; they are critical components of a successful deployment pipeline, allowing FusionCorp to confidently deliver new features while knowing they have a dependable and efficient mechanism to manage modifications. Progressive delivery, when done correctly, converts the deployment process into a controlled, adaptive, and feedback-driven cycle that is critical for sustaining high service quality and customer happiness.

CHAPTER 8: BUILDING MICRO PROXIES WITH RUST

Introduction to Rust Programming

Benefits of Rust

When we look at Rust's role in the development of Linkerd proxies, we can see that its characteristics match the needs of service mesh infrastructure perfectly. The language's emphasis on safety and efficiency is critical in this environment. Proxies play an important role in controlling communication between services in service meshes, therefore high-performance, dependable, and secure solutions are required.

Rust's approach to memory safety, via its ownership model, prevents typical memory issues, which is a significant advantage in proxy development where stability and security are crucial. Its concurrency management capabilities ensure that Rust-based proxies can manage concurrent requests rapidly and reliably, which is critical in high-traffic network situations. Rust's combination of low-level control over system resources and high-level abstractions makes it ideal for developing complicated network applications such as Linkerd proxies. This control allows you to fine-tune performance-critical components while keeping the code readable and manageable.

Furthermore, Rust's zero-cost abstractions ensure that these high-level abstractions do not degrade the application's runtime efficiency. This is especially important in a service mesh context, where each millisecond of latency matters. Rust's broad ecosystem, which includes the Cargo package manager and a developing library system, enables powerful development environments. This ecosystem makes it easier to design, manage, and deploy Rust applications, leading to faster development cycles for Linkerd proxies.

Why Rust for Linkerd Proxies?

The decision to use Rust for Linkerd proxies is based on its technical capabilities, particularly performance and safety. In service meshes, where proxies are critical for inter-service communication, Rust's efficiency and low latency are important. Unlike traditional system programming languages, which are prone to memory safety concerns, Rust maintains safety without using a garbage collector, avoiding usual speed constraints.

Rust's dependability is further enhanced by its strong type system and compiler checks, ensuring the resilience required for Linkerd proxies. Its concurrency approach effectively manages multiple simultaneous requests, which is a typical requirement in service meshes. The small footprint of Rust binaries makes them ideal for constructing lightweight microproxies.

The vibrant Rust community, which prioritizes safety and performance, as well as the developing ecosystem, notably in networking and asynchronous processing, provide a great platform for sophisticated proxy development. Rust's current features, such as pattern matching and strong error handling, help create maintainable and robust proxy software.

Setting up Rust Environment

Rust's installation is managed by a tool called rustup, which simplifies the process and also helps in managing Rust versions and associated tools.

Download and Install rustup

Open a Terminal
Access your Linux terminal. This can be done through your desktop environment or by accessing your server via SSH, depending on your setup.

Download and Install rustup
Run the following command in the terminal to download and install rustup:

```
curl --proto '=https' --tlsv1.2 -sSf https://sh.rustup.rs | sh
```

This command downloads a script and starts the installation process for rustup, which is the Rust toolchain installer.

Follow On-Screen Instructions
The script will direct you through the installation process. You'll be prompted to proceed with the default installation or customize it. For most users, the default installation is sufficient.

Update PATH Environment Variable

After installation, rustup will suggest you add the Rust toolchain to your PATH. This can be done by running:

```
source $HOME/.cargo/env
```

Alternatively, you can add the above line to your .bashrc or .bash_profile to ensure Rust is available in every session.

Verifying Installation

Check Rust Version
To verify that Rust is installed correctly, use:

```
rustc --version
```

This command displays the current version of Rust compiler (rustc), confirming the successful installation.

Test with a Simple Program
Create a simple Rust program to ensure everything is working. Write a "Hello, world!" program:
Create a new file named hello.rs.

Add the following Rust code to the file:

```
fn main() {
    println!("Hello, world!");
}
```

Compile the program by running:

```
rustc hello.rs
```

Run the compiled program:

```
./hello
```

If the output is "Hello, world!", Rust is installed and functioning correctly.

Update and Manage Versions

Updating Rust
Rust can be updated to the latest version using rustup. Simply run:

```
rustup update
```

This command checks for the latest version of Rust and updates the toolchain.

Managing Different Rust Versions
rustup allows you to manage multiple Rust versions. You can switch between stable, beta, and nightly versions of Rust depending on your needs.

With Rust installed, the simplicity of the installation process, combined with the robust tooling provided by rustup, ensures that FusionCorp's team can focus on leveraging Rust's capabilities in their service mesh infrastructure without worrying about the complexities of the language setup.

Understand Micro Proxies

Definition

Standard proxies are more general-purpose and feature-rich. They are designed to handle a wide range of networking tasks, including caching, authentication, and complex routing. Whereas, Micro proxies are lightweight, minimalistic proxies designed specifically for high-performance, low-resource environments like service meshes. Their primary focus is on speed and efficiency. They are optimized for a smaller set of functionalities compared to standard proxies, focusing mainly on the essential features required for service mesh operations like routing, load balancing, and basic security. Due to their minimalistic design, micro proxies have a smaller memory footprint and lower CPU usage. They are particularly adept at handling high-throughput and low-latency scenarios, which are common in microservices architectures.

Use in Service Mesh

In a service mesh, micro proxies are deployed as sidecars alongside service pods, handling the ingress and egress of network traffic for each service instance. This design allows for fine-grained control and observability of traffic.

Building Micro Proxies in Rust

To build micro proxies for Linkerd using Rust, the process involves several key steps:

Identify the Needs
Clearly define what functionalities are required for the micro proxy. Typically, this includes basic request routing, load balancing, TLS termination, and observability features.

Environment Setup
Ensure the Rust development environment is set up correctly. This includes having Rust, Cargo (Rust's package manager), and necessary dependencies installed.

Study Linkerd's Proxy Requirements
Understand how Linkerd's service mesh architecture works, especially how it interacts with proxies. This knowledge is key to ensuring that the micro proxy aligns well with Linkerd's operational paradigm.

Plan the Proxy Design
Decide on the architecture of the micro proxy. This involves determining how it will handle

requests, manage traffic routing, and implement security measures.

Coding the Proxy
Start coding the proxy in Rust. Leverage Rust's features like async/await for efficient network communication, and its strong type system for reliability. Implement essential features like HTTP request handling, TCP/UDP support, and integration points with Linkerd's control plane.

Unit and Integration Testing
Thoroughly test the proxy to ensure it meets the necessary performance and security standards. This includes both unit tests and integration tests within a Kubernetes environment. Performance optimization is crucial to ensure the proxy does not become a bottleneck in the service mesh.

Deploy with Linkerd
Once the proxy is developed and tested, integrate it with Linkerd. This involves deploying it as a sidecar proxy in a Kubernetes cluster where Linkerd is operational.

Iterate Based on Feedback
Continuously improve the proxy based on real-world usage feedback, performance metrics, and evolving requirements of the service mesh.

Building micro proxies for Linkerd in Rust aligns closely with the goals of optimizing network communication and enhancing the overall effectiveness of the service mesh infrastructure.

Building a Rust-based Micro Proxy

We shall walk through a simplified version of this process, focusing on the core elements that make up a basic micro proxy suitable for integration with Linkerd.

Create a New Project

Use Cargo, Rust's package manager, to create a new project.

In the terminal, run:

```
cargo new linkerd_micro_proxy
cd linkerd_micro_proxy
```

This command creates a new Rust project named linkerd_micro_proxy and navigates into the project directory.

Edit Cargo.toml

Open the Cargo.toml file in the project directory. Add necessary dependencies for HTTP handling and asynchronous programming. For example:

```
[dependencies]
hyper = "0.14"
tokio = { version = "1", features = ["full"] }
```

Writing the Proxy Server Code

Open src/main.rs and write a basic HTTP server. This server will act as the proxy, receiving requests and forwarding them.

Following is the sample code snippet for a basic HTTP server:

```
use hyper::{Body, Request, Response, Server};
use hyper::service::{make_service_fn, service_fn};
use std::net::SocketAddr;

async fn handle_request(_req: Request<Body>) -> Result<Response<Body>,
hyper::Error> {
    // Here, you would add the logic to handle the request and forward it
    Ok(Response::new("Hello, World!".into()))
}

#[tokio::main]
async fn main() {
    let addr = SocketAddr::from(([127, 0, 0, 1], 3000));

    let make_svc = make_service_fn(|_conn| async {
        Ok::<_, hyper::Error>(service_fn(handle_request))
```

```
    });

    let server = Server::bind(&addr).serve(make_svc);

    println!("Listening on http://{}", addr);

    if let Err(e) = server.await {
        eprintln!("server error: {}", e);
    }
}
```

This code sets up a basic HTTP server that listens on port 3000 and responds with "Hello, World!" to all requests.

Run the Proxy

In the terminal, start the proxy server using Cargo:

```
cargo run
```

Ensure it's listening on the specified port. Use a tool like curl to send requests to the proxy server and observe the responses.

Sidecar Deployment

Once the micro proxy is functional, the next step is to deploy it alongside a service in your Kubernetes cluster as a sidecar. Update the service's deployment configuration to include the micro proxy as an additional container. Do not forget to ensure Linkerd is configured to recognize and interact with your custom proxy. This might involve configuring service discovery to route traffic through your proxy.

While the above sample program creates a simple proxy, the key takeaway is understanding the process of building, testing, and deploying a Rust-based micro proxy, which can then be expanded upon and customized for specific requirements in a service mesh environment.

Integrate Rust Proxies into Linkerd

There are a number of stages involved in integrating the Rust micro proxy we wrote into the Linkerd service mesh such that it works flawlessly within the mesh design. We shall walk over the integration process and then learn about how to ensure that it's effective.

Containerize Micro Proxy

Create a Dockerfile

Write a Dockerfile to containerize the Rust-built micro proxy. The Dockerfile will compile the Rust application and prepare it for deployment.

Example Dockerfile:

```
FROM rust:1.48 as builder
WORKDIR /usr/src/myapp
COPY . .
RUN cargo install --path .

FROM debian:buster-slim
COPY --from=builder /usr/local/cargo/bin/myapp /usr/local/bin/myapp
CMD ["myapp"]
```

This Dockerfile uses a multi-stage build: the first stage builds the application, and the second stage prepares the runtime environment.

Build and Push the Docker Image

Build the Docker image using:

```
docker build -t myorg/myapp:latest .
```

Push the image to a container registry accessible to your Kubernetes cluster:

```
docker push myorg/myapp:latest
```

Deploy the Proxy as a Sidecar

Update Kubernetes Deployment

Modify the Kubernetes deployment YAML of the service you wish to add the proxy to. Add the micro proxy container as a sidecar.

Example snippet to include in the deployment YAML:

```
containers:
- name: myapp-proxy
  image: myorg/myapp:latest
  ports:
  - containerPort: 8080
```

This configuration adds the proxy as an additional container in the pod.

Configure Linkerd to Recognize the Proxy

Ensure that the Linkerd service mesh is configured to recognize and properly route traffic through your micro proxy. You might need to adjust the service and deployment configurations so that traffic intended for your service is intercepted by the micro proxy.

Deploy Changes to Kubernetes

Apply the changes to your Kubernetes cluster using:

```
kubectl apply -f deployment.yaml
```

Verifying Integration with Linkerd

Verify Pod Deployment

Ensure the pod with your service and the new proxy sidecar is running without issues.
Use kubectl get pods to check the status.

Inspect Linkerd Dashboard

Open the Linkerd dashboard to inspect the service. Check if the dashboard displays metrics for the service with the new proxy. Successful display of metrics indicates the proxy is part of the mesh.

Monitor Traffic

Send traffic to your service and observe using both Linkerd's dashboard and any logging or monitoring solutions you have in place. Look for successful routing through the micro proxy and check for any anomalies in response times or error rates.

Validate Network Policies

If you have Kubernetes network policies in place, validate that they allow traffic to and from your micro proxy as expected.

Simulate Failures

Test how your system behaves under failure scenarios. Ensure that the micro proxy correctly handles network issues, service downtime, and other potential problems. This step is crucial to confirm the resilience of your integration.

This integration enhances the network capabilities of your services within the mesh and also provides valuable insights into the performance and reliability of the proxy itself. It's a process that demands attention to detail, especially in ensuring seamless traffic flow and mesh compliance.

linkerd2-proxy

Introduction

linkerd2-proxy, the default proxy for Linkerd, is integral for routing network traffic within the service mesh. This proxy, crafted in Rust, harnesses the language's strengths in safety, performance, and handling concurrent operations. Its design focuses on maintaining low latency and minimal overhead to prevent any slowdown in service communication.

Key characteristics of linkerd2-proxy include its security-first approach, implementing mutual TLS automatically for all traffic, thus securing communication channels. It stands out in its detailed observability features, offering in-depth metrics such as request volumes, success rates, and latencies, essential for effective monitoring and troubleshooting. In terms of load balancing, linkerd2-proxy employs sophisticated algorithms to evenly distribute traffic among available service instances. Additionally, it's equipped with mechanisms for handling failures, including retries, timeouts, and circuit breaking. This proxy's versatility is further enhanced by its support for various protocols, including HTTP/1.x, HTTP/2, and gRPC, catering to diverse service communication needs.

linkerd2-proxy vs. Custom Rust-Built Micro Proxy

In comparing linkerd2-proxy with a custom Rust-built micro proxy, we notice both similarities and distinct differences, reflecting in their design and functionalities. linkerd2-proxy, as an integral

127

part of the Linkerd service mesh, is designed to align seamlessly with its ecosystem, featuring a comprehensive set of functionalities like advanced load balancing, automatic mTLS, and extensive protocol support. On the contrary, a custom Rust-built proxy is more tailored to specific needs, potentially requiring extra configuration for full Linkerd integration.

While linkerd2-proxy is optimized for high performance in a service mesh, ensuring minimal latency and overhead, a custom proxy's optimization level may vary based on its specific use case. The resource footprint of linkerd2-proxy might be slightly larger due to its extensive feature set, in contrast to a potentially leaner custom proxy.

The built-in security features, especially the automatic mTLS in linkerd2-proxy, provide robust security out-of-the-box, a feature that would demand additional effort in a custom-built proxy. Moreover, linkerd2-proxy benefits from extensive testing and stability checks within the Linkerd project, ensuring reliability.

Customization and flexibility are key in a custom-built proxy, allowing it to be fine-tuned for specific environmental needs. However, integrating such a proxy with Linkerd's control plane could necessitate additional steps, unlike the inherent design of linkerd2-proxy for seamless integration.

Utilize linkerd2-proxy in FusionCorp

The service mesh experience can be improved and made more streamlined by integrating linkerd2-proxy into FusionCorp's current setup. We can take advantage of linkerd2-proxy's enhanced load balancing, secure communication, and detailed observability thanks to this integration.

Review Existing Services

First, take a look at the current services running in the Kubernetes cluster. Identify services that will benefit most from linkerd2-proxy integration, such as those requiring secure communication, load balancing, or detailed monitoring.

Injecting linkerd2-proxy into Services

Automatic Proxy Injection

For new deployments, ensure automatic sidecar injection is enabled. This can be done by annotating the namespace with:

```
kubectl annotate namespace <namespace> linkerd.io/inject=enabled
```

With this, any new pod within the annotated namespace will automatically have the linkerd2-

proxy sidecar injected.

Manual Injection

For existing services, manually update the deployments to include linkerd2-proxy. Use:

```
kubectl get deploy -o yaml | linkerd inject - | kubectl apply -f -
```

This command retrieves the current deployments, injects the proxy, and then updates the deployments.

Configuring Traffic Routing

Create service profiles for your services to take advantage of linkerd2-proxy's per-route metrics, retries, and timeouts.

Use the Linkerd CLI to create a basic service profile:

```
linkerd profile --namespace <namespace> <service> --o yaml > <service-profile>.yaml
```

Modify the generated profile to define retry policies, timeout settings, and response classifications.

Enabling mTLS

By default, linkerd2-proxy enables mutual TLS (mTLS) for all communication between services in the mesh. Verify that mTLS is working as expected using:

```
linkerd -n <namespace> check --proxy
```

This command checks the proxy's status, including mTLS.

Dashboard Utilization

Use the Linkerd dashboard to observe the real-time metrics and health of your services. Access the dashboard with:

```
linkerd dashboard
```

The dashboard provides a comprehensive view of request volumes, success rates, and latencies.

For a more detailed view of a particular service, use the Linkerd CLI:

```
linkerd -n <namespace> stat deploy/<deployment>
```

Fine-Tuning Load Balancing and Traffic Management

Adjust load-balancing strategies as needed. For instance, you might prefer a least-request load balancer for certain services. These configurations can be adjusted in the linkerd2-proxy settings or the service profiles.

Use TrafficSplit resources for advanced traffic management, like canary deployments. Define the traffic splits to gradually shift traffic between different service versions.

Advanced Features

Retry and Timeout Policies

Implement retry and timeout policies in the service profiles to improve the resilience of your services. For example, add a retry policy for idempotent requests to automatically retry failed requests.

Configure Gateway and Ingress

If using an ingress controller, ensure it's configured to work with linkerd2-proxy. The ingress traffic should also be part of the mesh for complete observability and security.

This entire integration enhances the security, reliability, and observability of the services, while also providing advanced traffic management capabilities thereby ensuring services are not only highly available and resilient but also benefit from the sophisticated features that linkerd2-proxy offers.

Enable High Availability of Micro Proxies

It takes strategy to integrate high availability (HA) into the Rust-built micro proxy inside FusionCorp's service mesh with Linkerd. Even if there are interruptions or failures, the micro proxy will still be dependable and operational thanks to high availability. I'll show you, step by step, how to do this.

Begin by assessing the requirements for high availability. This includes determining the acceptable level of redundancy, failover mechanisms, and load distribution strategies.

Deploy Multiple Instances

Deploy multiple instances of the Rust-built micro proxy across different nodes in the Kubernetes cluster. This ensures that the failure of one node doesn't render the proxy service unavailable. Modify the deployment YAML to scale the number of proxy instances.

For example:

```
apiVersion: apps/v1
kind: Deployment
...
spec:
  replicas: 3
  ...
```

Configure Load Balancing
Set up a load balancer to distribute traffic evenly across the different instances of the micro proxy. Use Kubernetes services of type LoadBalancer or integrate an external load balancer if preferred.

Implement Health Checks
Implement robust health checks for the micro proxy. Kubernetes can use these health checks to understand the status of each proxy instance. Include liveness and readiness probes in the deployment configuration as below:

```
livenessProbe:
  httpGet:
    path: /health
    port: http
readinessProbe:
  httpGet:
    path: /ready
    port: http
```

Failover Strategies
Define and implement failover strategies. In Kubernetes, services will automatically reroute traffic away from unhealthy instances. Consider more sophisticated failover mechanisms if required, like

active/passive or active/active setups.

Configure DNS settings and network policies to ensure smooth traffic routing and failover. This may involve setting up DNS entries that point to the load balancer.

Conduct Failover Tests
Simulate failures of proxy instances and observe the behavior. Ensure traffic is appropriately rerouted and no significant disruption occurs. Test the recovery process to ensure proxy instances are correctly reinstated after failure.

And after all this, continuously gather metrics and feedback on the high availability setup. Look for potential bottlenecks or areas of improvement. Based on observations and data, make necessary adjustments to optimize high availability. This could involve scaling adjustments, network policy refinements, or tweaks to the load balancing setup.

This is the process that FusionCorp will follow to ensure that their Rust-built micro proxy is highly available within the Linkerd service mesh. Both the proxy's dependability and the service mesh infrastructure's overall robustness are guaranteed by this configuration.

Best Practices - Rust, Micro Proxies and linkerd2-proxy

Working with Rust, micro proxies, and linkerd2-proxy in a service mesh environment like Linkerd involves a blend of programming discipline, architectural understanding, and operational best practices. Following practices are crucial for optimizing performance, ensuring security, and maintaining the reliability of the service mesh.

Best Practices in Working with Rust

#1 - Emphasize Memory Safety
Rust's ownership model is a cornerstone of its memory safety guarantees. It's important to thoroughly understand and correctly use Rust's ownership, borrowing, and lifetimes concepts to prevent common errors like null pointer dereferences and buffer overflows.

#2 - Leverage Concurrency Features
Utilize Rust's powerful concurrency features, especially in the context of asynchronous programming. Rust's guarantees around data races are particularly beneficial when writing network applications like micro proxies.

#3 - Error Handling
Rust encourages robust error handling practices. Use Result and Option types effectively to handle potential errors and avoid unwrapping unless absolutely sure.

#4 - Code Testing and Coverage
Rigorously test Rust code. Unit tests, integration tests, and documentation tests (doctests) are essential to ensure that the code behaves as expected and remains maintainable and error-free.

Best Practices for Micro Proxies

#1 - Focus on Performance
Since micro proxies are a critical part of the service mesh, they need to be highly performant. Optimize for low latency and high throughput, and monitor performance metrics closely.

#2 - Keep It Lightweight
The key advantage of a micro proxy is its lightweight nature. Focus on including only necessary features to keep the proxy lean and efficient.

#3 - Scalability
Design micro proxies to be scalable. In a Kubernetes environment, they should be able to handle scaling up and down based on the load.

#4 - Security
Implement robust security measures. If the micro proxy handles traffic encryption and decryption, ensure that it adheres to the latest security standards and practices.

Best Practices with linkerd2-proxy

#1 - Integration with Linkerd
Ensure seamless integration of linkerd2-proxy with Linkerd's control plane. Proper configuration and regular updates are key to maintaining this integration.

#2 - Monitoring and Observability
Utilize Linkerd's extensive monitoring and observability features. Keep a close eye on metrics provided by linkerd2-proxy for traffic patterns, performance bottlenecks, and potential issues.

#3 - Regular Updates
Keep linkerd2-proxy updated to benefit from the latest features, performance improvements, and security patches.

While linkerd2-proxy works well out of the box, don't hesitate to customize its configuration to better suit the specific needs of your environment.

#5 - *Load Balancing and Traffic Management*
Experiment with and optimize linkerd2-proxy's load balancing and traffic management features to achieve the most efficient routing and failover behaviors.

Incorporating these best practices substantially benefit FusionCorp's service mesh implementation using Rust, micro proxies, and linkerd2-proxy, striking the right balance between leveraging Rust's powerful features for safety and performance, optimizing micro proxies for efficiency and scalability, and ensuring linkerd2-proxy is well-integrated and monitored within the Linkerd ecosystem.

Summary

This chapter went into great detail on Rust programming and how it may be used to create microproxies, notably for integration with Linkerd's service mesh. We began with an overview of Rust, stressing crucial aspects such as memory safety, concurrency management, and performance economy. These characteristics make Rust an excellent candidate for developing microproxies, which are critical components of a service mesh that handle network traffic effectively and securely. The chapter stressed Rust's ability to provide low-level control while keeping high-level abstractions, making it powerful and useful for system-level development.

We investigated the characteristics of micro proxies and compared them to normal proxies, highlighting their lightweight and high-performance nature, which is appropriate for service mesh contexts. The focus then switched to a step-by-step instruction to creating a rudimentary micro proxy in Rust. This procedure included creating a Rust project, implementing a simple HTTP server, and adding necessary proxy functionality. While our proxy was simple, it served as a foundation for comprehending the complexity of such an attempt. We also highlighted how to integrate these custom-built proxies into FusionCorp's existing Linkerd configuration, including containerization, deployment, and high availability. The impact of linkerd2-proxy, Linkerd's default proxy, was also investigated. We studied its full feature set, which is intended to work seamlessly within the Linkerd ecosystem, and compared it to our custom Rust-built micro proxy to better understand the trade-offs between a general-purpose proxy and one suited to specific purposes.

The chapter finished with a set of best practices for Rust programming, micro proxy creation, and using linkerd2-proxy. These techniques stressed memory safety, error handling, performance optimization, and integration and monitoring inside the Linkerd service mesh. Adhering to these guidelines guarantees that FusionCorp's service mesh infrastructure remains strong, efficient, and secure, exploiting Rust's strengths and the specialized capabilities of microproxies to improve network architecture.

Thank You

Index

O

P

R

S

T

V

Z

Epilogue

As our journey through the complex world of service meshes and Linkerd comes to a close, I find myself reflecting on the evolution of this technology and its influence. Writing this book has been a trip not only through the technical landscapes of service meshes, but also through their revolutionary possibilities for organisations navigating the difficulties of cloud-native settings.

We began with the fundamentals, explaining the importance of service meshes, and then on to the capabilities and functionalities of Linkerd. Along the way, we looked at the practical aspects of deploying and administering a service mesh, learned about the complexities of Rust for creating efficient microproxies, and discovered solutions for advanced traffic control and availability.

What I really want you to get out of this book isn't only a solid grounding in Linkerd and service meshes. It's the recognition that, in the face of fast expanding technology, continuous learning and adaptability are essential for mastering complexity. The chapters in this book serve as more than just guides; they are stepping stones to creating more robust, efficient, and secure systems.

As you implement what you've learned, keep in mind that technology is continuously changing. What appears cutting-edge today could become the foundation tomorrow. Embrace change and use the information you've gathered to tackle current problems as well as develop for the future.

Finally, I want to thank you for accompanying me on this instructive voyage. May the information you've received from these pages enable you and your teams to fully realize the promise of Linkerd and service meshes, paving the way for more resilient, scalable, and efficient cloud-native solutions.

Made in the USA
Las Vegas, NV
31 August 2024

94621429R00087